A is Adorable

26 A to Z Animal Alphabet Quilts & Crafts for Baby

LANDAUER BOOKS

A is Adorable

Copyright© 2005 by Landauer Corporation
Projects Copyright© 2005 by Janet Wecker-Frisch

This book was designed, produced, and published by Landauer Books
A division of Landauer Corporation
3100 NW 101st Street, Urbandale, IA 50322

President/Publisher: Jeramy Lanigan Landauer
Director of Operations: Kitty Jacobson
Editor in Chief: Becky Johnston
Creative Director: Laurel Albright
Contributing Writer: Connie McCall
Technical Writers: Ann Regal, Rhonda Matus
Technical Illustrator: Linda Bender
Editorial Assistants: Debby Burgraff, Judy Hunsicker
We also wish to thank Elizabeth Cecchettini, Nancy Nigh
and Nancy McClellan for their project creations and sewing.
Photographer: Craig Anderson Photography

Library of Congress Cataloging-in-Publication Data

Wecker-Frisch, Janet.
  A is adorable : 26 animal alphabet quilts & crafts for baby / [Janet Wecker-Frisch]
    p. cm.
  Includes index.
  ISBN 1-890621-85-4 (alk. paper)
  1. Patchwork--Patterns. 2. Quilting--Patterns. 3. Crib quilts. 4. Alphabet in art. I. Title.
TT835.W415 2005   03285-2441   10/06
746.46'041--dc22

2005044126

This book printed on acid-free paper.
Printed in USA

ISBN 13: 978-1-890621-85-8
ISBN 10:   1-890621-85-4

10-9-8-7-6-5-4-3-2-1

Introduction

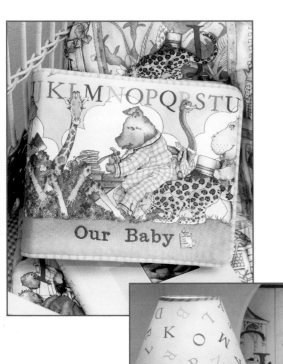

Discover how easy it is to create your own charming gift and nursery collection inspired by the whimsical Hungry Animal Alphabet© illustrations and fabrics designed by artist Janet Wecker-Frisch.

For fun and imaginative décor for your baby, Janet Wecker-Frisch has designed one of the most delightful fabric lines ever. Janet's paintings of Hungry Animal Alphabet© characters featured in a fabric collection from South Sea Imports® take center stage in the pages of this book. Each animal painting—from Ali the Gator to Zach the Zebra is accompanied by a project that is perfect for baby shower gift-giving or for a coordinated nursery ensemble.

Choose from 26 animal alphabet quilts and crafts for baby including a crib-size and a twin-size quilt, panel wallhanging, diaper stacker, growth chart, mobile, pillows, rugs, shadow boxes, toys and games that offer more than a dozen decorating ideas for baby's room.

Thanks to Janet's creative menagerie of painted animals from A to Z, on the following pages you'll find projects that are fabulous, fast, and sure to bring smiles to all who see them.

About the Artist

Inspired by her father, talented artist, Janet Wecker-Frisch has been drawing and painting since childhood. She translated her irresistible watercolor illustrations into her own line of ceramic ornaments. Their success led to licenses for wallpaper and border décor, and fabrics. Janet's Hungry Animal Alphabet© characters are the inspiration for a fabric collection created for South Sea Imports®. On the drawing board are more whimsical collections from Janet Wecker-Frisch including Mother Goose storybook characters, snowmen, and Noah's Ark. Janet paints in a studio in her home which she shares with her husband, David. Located in House Springs, Missouri, a suburb of St. Louis, their home is often frequented by visits from their grown children—David, Jacqueline, Katie—and granddaughters—Kaylan and Sydney.

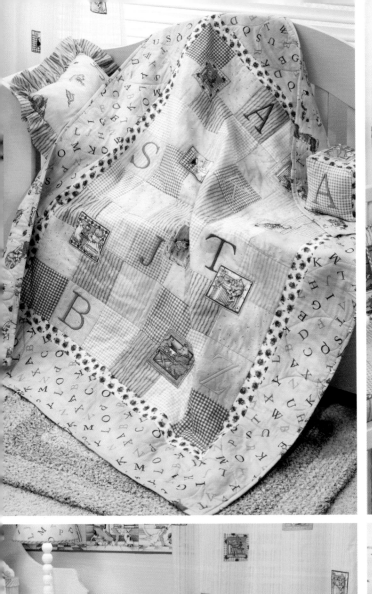

Contents

◆◆◆◆

Ali the Gator

A is for Alphabet Quilt

*Creating a crib-size quilt for the nursery is as easy as ABC.
Start with pastel gingham prints and checks that coordinate with
charming animals and alphabet letters from Janet Wecker-Frisch.*

Alphabet Quilt

Crib Quilt

Finished size: 43x50"

Materials

- Fabric with motif squares and rectangles for appliqués

- 1/4 yard each of check fabric in blue, green, pink, red, and yellow for center squares

- 1/4 yard each of small floral print fabric in blue, green, pink, and yellow for center squares

- 1/4 yard each of stripe fabric in blue, green, and yellow for center squares

- 1/4 yard of cream floral print fabric for inner border

- 1-5/8 yards of green print fabric for outer border

- 1-3/4 yards of blue print fabric for backing and binding

- 48x60" piece of quilt batting

- Sulky® Tear-Easy™ Stabilizer

- Sulky® KK 2000 temporary spray adhesive

- Sulky® Rayon or Poly Deco™ Decorative Thread in blue, green, red, white, and yellow

- Sulky® Puffy Foam™ in blue, green, red, and yellow

- Paper-backed fusible webbing

- Sulky® Polyester Invisible Thread

- Template plastic

All measurements include 1/4" seam allowances.
Sew with right sides together unless otherwise specified.
The border strips are cut longer than needed and trimmed later to allow for individual differences in piecing.

Cut the Fabric

From motif fabric, cut:

> 8 motif squares or rectangles, leaving about 1/2" around each shape

From the 1/4 yard fabrics, cut:

> 8—8" letter squares (we cut 2 blue, 4 green, 1 pink, and 1 yellow)
> 40—5-1/4" center squares (we cut 8 blue, 7 green, 11 pink, 4 red, and 10 yellow)

From cream floral, cut:

> 4—2x44" inner border strips

From green print, cut:

> 2—6-1/4x35" outer border strips
> 2—6-1/4x56" outer border strips

From blue print, cut:

> 1—44x56" backing rectangle
> 5—1-1/2x44" binding strips

Instructions

Assemble the Quilt Center

1. Cut sixteen 8" squares of tear-away stabilizer. Use temporary spray adhesive to center two layers of stabilizer on the back of each 8" letter square. Machine-embroider a 3-1/4"-tall letter centered on each of the stabilized squares using decorative thread and matching Puffy Foam. Refer to the photo and Quilt Assembly Diagram for ideas on combining thread and fabric colors. Tear away the stabilizer. Trim each embroidered square into a 5-1/4" square, centering the letter. For more information about embroidering, refer to "E is for Embroidered Accents" on page 28.

2. Lay out the center blocks on a flat surface, including the embroidered letter squares, in 8 rows of 6 blocks, using one letter square in each row. Arrange the blocks as desired or use the Quilt Assembly Diagram as a guide.

3. When you are pleased with the arrangement, sew the blocks together in rows. Press the seam allowances of each row to one side, alternating the direction with each row.

4. Sew the rows together to complete the quilt center.

5. For each motif square or rectangle, cut a corresponding shape of fusible webbing. Fuse webbing to the wrong side of each shape, following the manufacturer's instructions. Carefully cut out the shapes. Remove the paper backing.

6. Spread the quilt center right side up on a flat surface. Referring to the Quilt Assembly Diagram, position the appliqué shapes on the quilt, centering each over an intersection of four squares. When you are happy with the arrangement, pin the shapes in place. Fuse the shapes in place.

7. Cut pieces of tear-away stabilizer slightly larger than the fused shapes. Center a piece of stabilizer behind each fused shape on the back of the quilt center with temporary spray adhesive. Satin-stitch over the edges of each shape with white decorative thread. For an added touch, use a second color of decorative thread to machine-buttonhole stitch directly over the white satin stitching. Tear away the stabilizer.

Assemble the Quilt Top

1. Measure to find the length of the quilt center through the center as shown in Diagram A. Cut two 2"-wide cream floral inner border strips to this length. Sew the inner borders to the left and right edges of the quilt center. Press the seam allowances toward the borders.

Diagram A

2. Measure the quilt width through the center, including the borders as shown in Diagram B. Cut two cream floral inner border strips to this length. Sew the inner borders to the top and bottom edges of the quilt. Press the seam allowances toward the borders.

Diagram B

3. Using the length found in Step 2, cut two outer borders from the 6-1/4"-wide green print strips. Referring to the Quilt Assembly Diagram, sew the outer borders to the top and bottom edges of the quilt. Press the seam allowances toward the outer borders.

4. Measure the quilt length through the center, including all borders. Trim the two remaining green print outer borders to this length. Sew the borders to the left and right edges of the quilt. Press the seam allowances toward the outer borders.

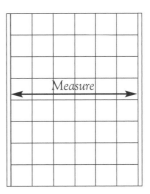
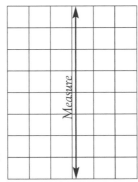

Complete the Crib Quilt

1. Smooth out the backing on a flat surface with the wrong side up and center the batting on the backing. Center the quilt top, right side up, on top of the batting. Baste the layers together.

2. Thread your machine with Sulky Polyester Invisible Thread in both the needle and the bobbin. Machine-quilt through all layers beginning in the center and working out to the edges. Refer to Diagram C to quilt between the vertical and horizontal rows of center squares. Quilt around each appliqué block and in the ditch along the outer edges of the quilt center and the outer edges of the inner border. Use the heart pattern and template plastic to quilt the outside border.

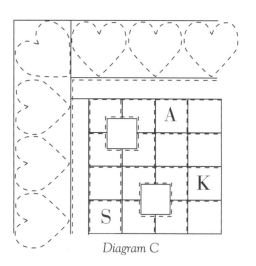

Diagram C

3. Sew the short ends of the binding strips together with diagonal seams to form one long binding strip. Trim the excess fabric, leaving 1/4" seam allowances. Press the seam allowances open. Fold the strip in half lengthwise with wrong sides together; press.

4. Beginning at the center of one edge of the quilt, place the binding strip on the right side of the quilt top, aligning the raw edges of the binding with the raw edges of the quilt top. Fold over the beginning of the binding strip about 1/2". Sew through all layers 1/4" from the raw edges, mitering the corners. Trim away the excess binding, leaving 1/2" at the end to overlap the beginning of the strip. Trim the batting and backing even with the quilt top.

5. Fold the binding to the back of the quilt to cover the machine stitching; press. Slip-stitch the folded edge of the binding in place or sew in the ditch along the binding, catching the folded edge of binding on the back of quilt.

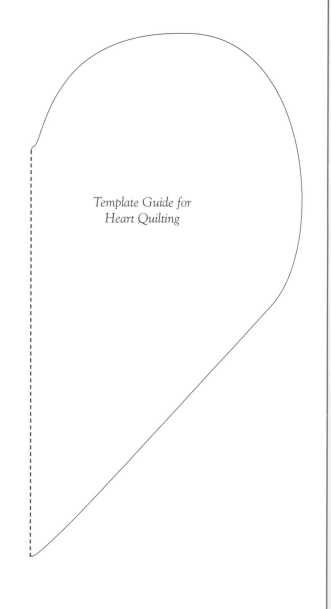

Template Guide for
Heart Quilting

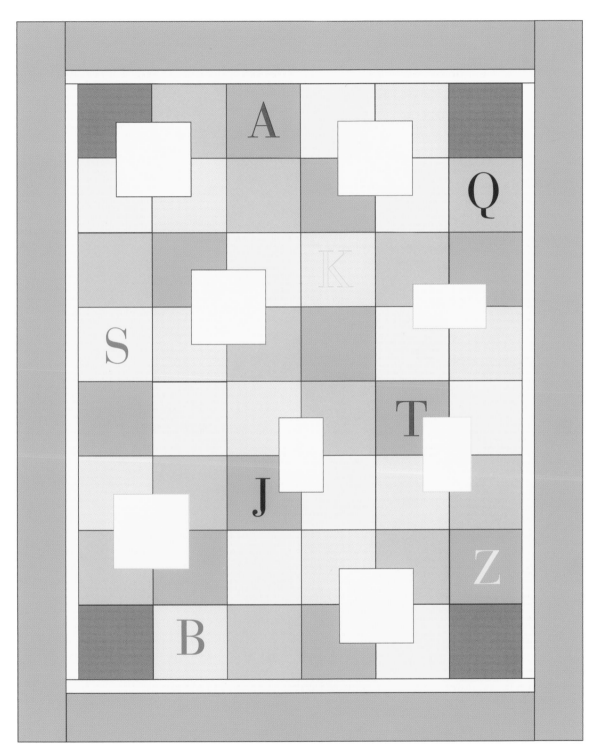

Crib Quilt Assembly Diagram

Bessie the Bear

B is for Baby's Buffet

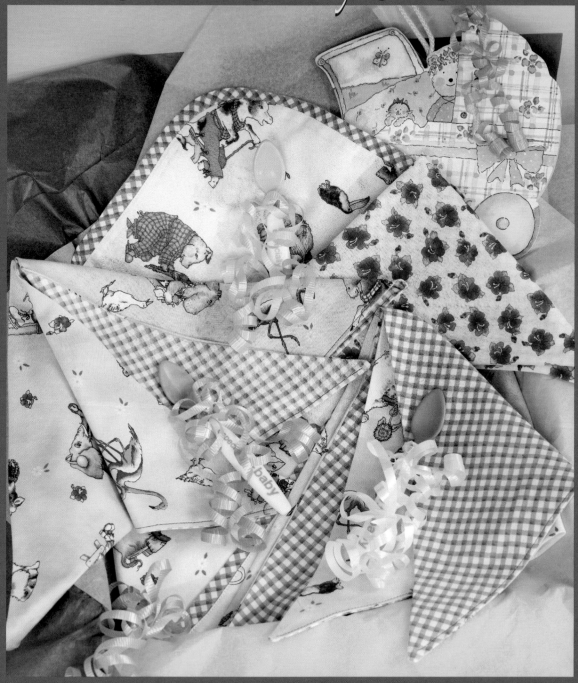

All set for the baby's buffet. This easy-to-sew kerchief bib is handy protection for Mom's shoulder or baby's shirt. The animal print reverses to a cheerful check. Add baby spoons for a shower gift duo.

Baby's Buffet

Bibs & Burps

Materials

◆ For a two-print reversible bib:
23" square each of two coordinating fabrics

◆ 1-1/2x50" bias strip of coordinating print fabric
for trim (optional)

◆ For a one-print reversible bib:
23" square of fabric

◆ 1-1/2x50" bias strip of coordinating print fabric
for trim (optional)

All measurements include 1/4" seam allowances.
Sew with right sides together unless otherwise specified.

Cut the Fabric

For a two-print bib, fold each square in half diagonally.
Cut on the fold, creating two triangles of each fabric.
Use one of each for a bib.

Instructions

1. Place two fabric triangles right sides together, or
   fold the 23" square in half diagonally with right
   sides together.

2. For optional trim, fold the 1-1/2" bias strip in
   half lengthwise with wrong sides together; press.
   Pin trim between the fabric layers along both 23"
   edges, aligning the raw edges. Curve the trim to
   round the corner at the bottom of the bib and
   let the trim extend at the ends of the long edge
   as shown in Diagram A. Trim the bib fabric to
   follow the curve of the trim at the center bottom
   of the bib.

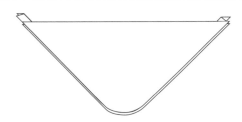

Diagram A

3. Sew the raw edges together, leaving a 3" opening in
   the long edge of the two-print bib and a 3" opening
   in a 23" edge of the one-print bib. Clip corners,
   turn right side out, and press.

4. For two-print bib, top-stitch 1/8" from the long
   edge, closing the opening in the stitching. For one-
   print bib, edge-stitch along both 23" edges of the
   bib as shown in Diagram B, closing the opening.

Diagram B

Choose from a two-print or one-print reversible bib style dressed up with a bias strip of coordinating print fabric for trim, if desired. Serve it all up with beribboned spoons for baby's buffet.

Clarence the Cow

C is for Crib Critters

What a dramatic focus for the nursery—a coordinating set of bumper pad, crib skirt, and simple-to-sew crib sheet. They're fun to make while waiting for the Big Day, and fun to give as a baby shower gift.

Crib Critters

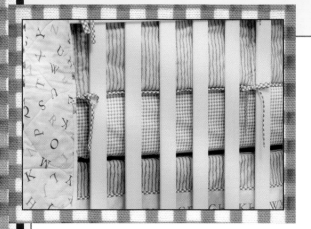

Crib Sheet

Materials

◆ 2 yards of green check fabric

◆ 1-1/4 yards of 1/4"-wide elastic

◆ Air-erasable marking pen

Cut the Fabric

From green check, cut:

    1—43x66" rectangle for sheet

Instructions

1. Fold the green check sheet rectangle in half lengthwise and then fold in half widthwise. Refer to Diagram A to curve the corners of the sheet. Working on the top layer of fabric, use an air-erasable marking pen to make a mark on each raw edge of fabric 8" from the corner without folds. Draw a curved line connecting the two marks. Cut through all layers along the curved line.

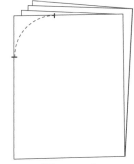

Diagram A

2. Press under 1/4" and then 5/8" on all raw edges of the sheet.

3. Sew close to the inner pressed edge to form a casing, leaving 1" openings on the long edges of the sheet 8 inches from each corner as shown in Diagram B.

Diagram B

4. Cut the elastic in half. Thread a length of elastic through the casing at one short end of the sheet. Secure the elastic ends in the casing with small straight stitches. Repeat with remaining length of elastic at opposite end of sheet.

5. Close the four openings, continuing the stitching lines of the casing.

Crib Skirt

Materials

◆ 2-1/4 yards of green stripe fabric for base and border

◆ 1-3/4 yards of bumper border fabric for skirt, with four usable borders per width of fabric

◆ 1/2 yard of red check fabric for trim

All measurements include 1/2" seam allowances.
Sew with right sides together unless otherwise specified.

Cut the Fabric

From green stripe, cut:
    1—28x52" base rectangle
    4—4x30-1/2" side border strips
    2—4x36" end border strips

From bumper border, cut:
    2—11x60" side skirt strips
    2—11x36" end skirt strips

From red check, cut:
    1-1/2"-wide bias strips to total 195" of trim

Instructions

1. Sew the short ends of the 1-1/2"-wide red check trim strips together to create one long strip. Press the seam allowances open. Cut the strip into two 36" lengths for the end skirts and two 60" lengths for the side skirts. Fold the trim strips in half lengthwise with wrong sides together; press.

2. Sew the short ends of two 4x30-1/2" green stripe side border strips together to make a 60" strip. Press the seam allowances open. Repeat for the remaining two side border strips.

3. With right sides together, align the top edge of an 11x36" end skirt strip with a long edge of a 4x36" green stripe border strip. Pin a 36"-long trim strip between the fabric layers, aligning the raw edges. Sew the raw edges together. Machine-overcast the seam allowance edges together. Press the seam allowances toward the green stripe border and the trim toward the bottom on the front of the skirt.

4. Machine-overcast the right, bottom and left edges of the pieced skirt. To hem, press under 1/2" on the overcast edges and top-stitch 3/8" from pressed edges.

5. Repeat Steps 3 and 4 for the remaining end skirt and for both 60" side skirts.

6. Using an air-erasable fabric marker, measure and mark the center of each raw edge of the skirt base, as shown in Diagram A, and the center of each top edge of the pieced side and end skirts.

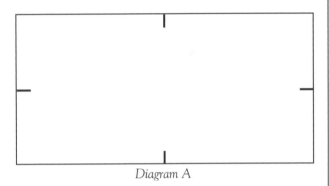

Diagram A

7. To make a box pleat, mark 4" on each side of the center mark of an end skirt as shown in Diagram B. Fold the skirt so the 4" marks meet at the center mark, leaving excess fabric on the wrong side of the skirt as shown in Diagram C. Press the pleat and baste along the top edge of pleat. Repeat for the remaining end skirt and each side skirt.

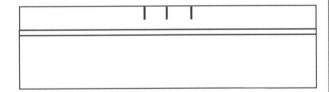

Diagram B

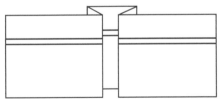

Diagram C

8. With wrong sides together, pin a side skirt to a corresponding edge of the skirt base, matching the center marks. Sew the side skirt to the base. Repeat for the remaining side skirt and each end skirt. Machine overcast the seam allowances together.

Crib Bumper Pad

Finished size: 9-3/4x180"

Materials

◆ Preprinted alphabet block quilt panel for appliqué

◆ 2 yards of green stripe fabric

◆ 1-1/2 yards of red check fabric

◆ 1/3 yard of green small floral fabric

◆ 1/3 yard of pink small floral fabric

◆ 1/3 yard of green check fabric

◆ 1/3 yard of pink check fabric

◆ 1/3 yard of blue check fabric

◆ 1/3 yard of blue stripe fabric

◆ 1/3 yard of yellow small floral fabric

◆ 1/3 yard of yellow stripe fabric

◆ 2/3 yard of 90"-wide high loft batting

◆ 11 yards of narrow cotton cording

◆ Sulky® Tear-Easy™ stabilizer

◆ Sulky® KK 2000 temporary spray adhesive

◆ Sulky® Puffy Foam™ in blue, green, red, and yellow

◆ Sulky® Rayon or Poly Deco™ thread in coordinating blue, green, red, and yellow

◆ Paper-backed fusible webbing

◆ Sulky® Polyester Invisible Thread

All measurements include 1/2" seam allowances.
Sew with right sides together unless otherwise specified.

Cut the Fabric

From quilt panel, cut:
> 4—6-1/4" alphabet block squares

From green stripe, cut:
> 6—10-3/4x30-1/4" back rectangles
> 2—10-3/4" front squares

From red check, cut:
> 1-1/2"-wide bias strips to equal 19 yards for piping and ties

From green small floral, cut:
> 2—12" letter squares

From pink small floral, cut:
> 2—12" letter squares

From each of the remaining 1/3 yard fabrics, cut:
> 2—10-3/4" front squares

From batting, cut:
> 2—10-3/4x90" strips

From fusible webbing, cut:
> 4—6-1/4" squares

Instructions

Assemble the Front

1. Cut eight 12" squares of tear-away stabilizer. Use temporary spray adhesive to center two layers of stabilizer on the back of each 12" green and pink letter square. Machine-embroider a 5"-tall letter centered on each of the stabilized squares using decorative thread and matching Puffy Foam. Embroider a red letter and a yellow letter on the green squares. Embroider a blue letter and a green letter on the pink squares. Tear away the stabilizer. Trim each embroidered square into a 10-3/4" square, centering the letter. For more information about embroidering, refer to "E is for Embroidered Accents" on page 28.

2. Sew together the 10-3/4" yellow floral and blue stripe squares and the blue check and green stripe squares in pairs as shown in Diagram A. Press all seam allowances open.

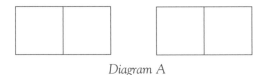

Diagram A

3. Fuse a square of webbing to the wrong side of each 6-1/4" alphabet block square, following the manufacturer's instructions. Remove the paper backing. Center an alphabet block on each pair of 10-3/4" squares from Step 2 as shown in Diagram B. Fuse the blocks in place.

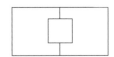

Diagram B

4. Use temporary spray adhesive to center an 8" square of tear-away stabilizer behind the fused block on the back of each square pair. Satin-stitch over the edges of each alphabet block with red decorative thread. Tear away the stabilizer.

Diagram C

5. Refer to Diagram C and the instructions that follow to sew together the 10-3/4" squares. Begin with a green check, followed by a yellow floral/blue stripe pair, pink check, green embroidered, yellow stripe, blue check/green stripe pair, pink embroidered, green check, yellow floral/blue stripe pair, pink check, green embroidered, yellow stripe, blue check/green stripe pair, and end with a pink embroidered square.

6. Sew the short ends of the red check piping strips together to form two 178" piping strips. Press the seam allowances open. Center cording on the wrong side of each strip and fold fabric over the cording, matching long edges. Use a zipper foot to sew through both fabric layers close to the cording.

7. Pin a piping strip along each long edge on the right side of the pieced front so the piping stitching is on the 1/2" seam line. Baste piping to the front using a zipper foot.

8. From the remaining red check bias strips, cut thirty-two 10" lengths for ties. Fold each tie strip in half lengthwise with right sides together. Sew with a 1/4" seam allowance, leaving one short edge open for turning. Trim the seam allowance to 1/8", turn right side out, and press.

9. Pin the ties to the right side of the pieced front where indicated by dots in Diagram D, aligning the raw edges. Place a single tie at each corner of the pieced front and pairs of ties at all remaining dots. Sew the ties in place.

Diagram D

Complete the Bumper Pad

1. Sew together the short edges of the 10-3/4x30-1/4" back rectangles to make one long back. Press the seam allowances open.

2. Place batting on the wrong side of the back, overlapping the short edges of the batting at the center of the back. Baste a scant 1/2" from the edges and trim the batting close to the stitching.

3. Pin pieced front to back with right sides together. Sew front to back, leaving one short edge open. Turn right side out and slip-stitch the opening closed.

4. Thread your sewing machine with Sulky Polyester Invisible Thread in both the needle and the bobbin. Machine-quilt through all layers at each vertical seam of the front squares; do not quilt at the center of the appliquéd pairs.

Duke the Donkey

D is for Diaper Stacker

"Where, oh, where do the diapers go?
Into our stacker, all in a row!"
A quilted lining and a firm base help the stacker keep its shape.

Diaper Stacker

Materials

◆ 1-1/3 yards of green print for lining

◆ 1 yard of green check fabric for body and facing

◆ 5/8 yard of red check fabric for piping and ties

◆ 1/4 yard of floral print fabric for trim

◆ 1/8 yard of green stripe fabric for center front

◆ 3 yards of narrow cotton cording

◆ 25x47" piece of lightweight batting

◆ 9x14-1/2" rectangle of extra-stiff felt for the base

◆ Sulky® Polyester Invisible Thread

All measurements include 1/4" seam allowances.
Sew with right sides together unless otherwise specified.

Cut the Fabric

From green print, cut:
    1—24x46" body lining rectangle
    1—9x14-1/2" base lining rectangle

From green check, cut:
    1—24x39" body rectangle
    1—9x14-1/2" base rectangle
    2—1-1/2x24" front facing bias strips

From red check, cut:
    4—1-1/4x24" piping bias strips
    4—2-1/2x18" tie strips

From floral print, cut:
    2—3x24" trim strips

From green stripe, cut:
    2—1-1/2x24" center front strips

Instructions

Assemble the Body

1. To make piping, cut the cording into four 24" lengths. Center a length of cording on the wrong side of a 1-1/4"-wide red check bias strip. Fold fabric over cording, matching long edges. Use a zipper foot to sew through both fabric layers close to the cording. Repeat for the remaining red check piping strips. Baste a piping length to each long edge of the 3x24" floral trim strips with raw edges facing out.

2. With right sides together, sew a green stripe center front strip to one long edge of each floral strip, sandwiching the piping between the layers. Press the seam allowances toward the floral strip.

3. Sew each remaining long edge of the floral strips to a 24" edge of the 24x39" green check body rectangle. Press the seam allowances toward the floral strips.

4. Place the 24x46" green print body lining right side down on a flat surface. Center the batting over the lining. Center the assembled body of the diaper stacker, right side up, on the batting. Baste the layers together.

5. Thread your sewing machine with Sulky Polyester Invisible Thread. Machine-quilt the green check area in a 2" diagonal grid as shown in Diagram A. Trim the batting even with the fabric edges.

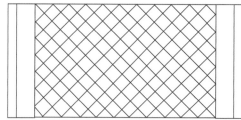

Diagram A

6. Press under 1/4" on one long edge of a 1-1/2x24" green check front facing. Sew the opposite edge to the center front strip. Fold the facing to the lining, covering the machine stitching; press. Slip-stitch the pressed edge of the facing in place or sew in the ditch along the piping, catching the pressed facing edge in place. Repeat with remaining front facing.

Add the Base

1. With wrong sides together, layer the 9x14-/12" green check base and green print lining with the felt in between. Baste the layers together. Machine-quilt the base in a 2" diagonal grid using invisible thread.

2. Mark the center of one long edge of the base. With right sides together, pin the base to the body, placing the center front edges of the body at the mark on the base. Referring to Diagram B, sew the base to the body, using a serge-stitch or sew a 1/4" seam and overcast the edges together.

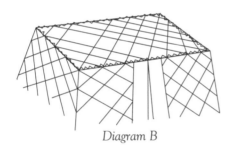

Diagram B

Complete the Diaper Stacker

1. To make a tie, fold a 2-1/2x18" red check strip in half lengthwise with right sides together. Diagonally trim one end of the folded strip as shown in Diagram C. Sew, leaving the short straight edge open. Turn the tie right side out and press. Repeat for the remaining ties.

Diagram C

2. Mark the center of the body's top edge; this is the top center back of the diaper stacker. With the diaper stacker inside out, bring the front edges of the body to the center back mark and pin. Continue pinning the top edges together, stopping 4" from the ends as shown in Diagram D. Align the raw ends of two ties. Insert the tie pair between the layers and pin in the top edge about 3-1/4" from the center front opening. Repeat for the remaining two ties. Baste the pinned area together, catching the ties in the stitching.

3. Refer to Diagram E to make end pleats. Bring the fold

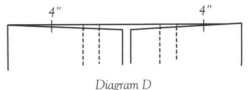

Diagram D

at one end of the top edge to the point where basting stops, folding fabric into a 2"-wide pleat on both the front and back of the diaper stacker; pin. Repeat for the fold at the opposite end. Serge-stitch the entire top edge or sew a 1/4" seam and overcast the edges together. Sew again 1/4" below the previous stitching line, reinforcing each end with backstitching. Trim the corners diagonally.

Diagram E

4. Turn the diaper stacker right side out. Tack the center front opening edges together 3" below the top edge.

Edgar the Elephant

Elephant Evening Eggplant Earmuffs Eyelet Eagerly Eats Edible

E is for Embroidered Accents

Embroidered accents will personalize almost anything.
Our basic instructions offer tips for easy machine-embroidered letters
and border accents for quilts, pillows, and soft toys.

Embroidered Accents

Machine Embroidery Basics

Materials

◆ Fabric to be embroidered

◆ Sulky® Tear-Easy™ stabilizer

◆ Sulky® KK 2000 temporary spray adhesive

◆ Chalk or air-erasable marker

◆ Sulky® 40 wt. Rayon or Poly Deco™ Decorative Thread

◆ 2mm-thick Sulky® Puffy Foam™ to match decorative thread

Instructions

1. Cut your fabric at least 1" larger than the desired finished size. This will enable you to trim the fabric to the desired size after the embroidery is complete, ensuring that the letter can be centered on the fabric.

2. To stabilize the fabric, cut two pieces of tear-away stabilizer the same size as the fabric. Spray a light coat of temporary spray adhesive between the two layers of stabilizer. Spray the top layer of stabilizer and place the fabric, wrong side down, on the top layer. Smooth all layers together.

3. Mark the center of the fabric with chalk or air-erasable marker. Hoop the fabric, following the machine manufacturer's instructions. The fabric should be taut. Take care not to pull or distort the fabric when hooping.

4. Select an embroidery letter style with wide satin columns. Outline font styles are a good choice because they are fully enclosed with no open ends on the columns. Another option is tapering open ends.

5. Place hooped fabric on the machine, aligning the foot with the center mark. Cut a piece of Puffy Foam slightly larger than the area to be embroidered. Place the Puffy Foam under the foot and lightly hold it in place until the first few stitches tack it in place. Or, apply a light coat of temporary spray adhesive to the back of the Puffy Foam before placing it on the hooped fabric. Stitch through all layers.

6. When the embroidery is complete, remove the hoop from the machine. Carefully tear away the excess Puffy Foam along the perforations made by the stitching. If the embroidered design has areas without perforations from stitching, use a scissors to trim the Puffy Foam close to the embroidery. To shrink little fuzzies of Puffy Foam along the edges of the embroidery, hold a steam iron about 1/2" above them and shoot them with steam.

The embroidered letters on this charming Hungry Animal Alphabet© ensemble were sewn with a computerized embroidery machine. Extra dimension was added to give the letters a padded look using Sulky Puffy Foam™. The Puffy Foam™ perforates cleanly when stitched through, and makes the stitching stand well above the fabric. Before embroidering the block, test sew over an extra piece of Puffy Foam™ on a scrap of stabilized fabric.

Frances, Fern, Frank & Ferdinand
the
Four Flamingos

F is for Framed Friends

Inexpensive wooden frames with fabric-covered mats become colorful, customized settings for a child's photo or favorite animal friends. To create charming nursery decor, group several framed "portraits" for greater impact.

Framed Friends

Framed Friends
Materials

◆ 8x10" picture frame with a mat

◆ 1/3 yard of check or floral print fabric for mat

◆ 1-1/4 yards of 1-1/2" bias strips of coordinating fabric for optional trim

◆ Large-print fabric with motif of your choice

◆ Spray-mount adhesive

◆ Fabric glue

Instructions

1. Remove the mat from the frame. Lay the mat down on the wrong side of the mat fabric. Draw around the outer edges of the mat. Cut the fabric 1" beyond the outer drawn lines.

2. Spray adhesive on the front of the mat, following the manufacturer's instructions. With the adhesive side down, center and press the mat on the wrong side of the mat fabric. Turn over and press the fabric onto the mat, smoothing out any wrinkles.

3. For the mat opening, draw a large X on the fabric from the inside corners as shown in Diagram A. Cut on the drawn lines. Then trim the fabric 1" from the inside edges of the mat.

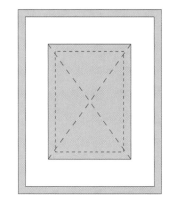

Diagram A

4. Wrap the trimmed fabric edges around the inside edges of the mat and glue to the back. Check the front and smooth out any puckers before the glue dries.

5. Trim the fabric at the outer corners at a diagonal, very close to the mat, as shown in Diagram B. Fold the fabric around the outside edges of the mat and glue to the back.

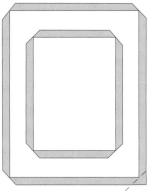

Diagram B

6. To add optional contrasting trim, press under 3/8" on each long edge of the 1-1/2"-wide bias strip. The trim should be 3/4" wide. Referring to the photo on page 33, cut a length of trim for each edge of the mat opening, adding 1" to secure on the back. Beginning at the center of the right edge of the mat opening, center and glue the corresponding trim in place. Take care to align or slightly overlap the mat fabric with the trim. Glue the trim ends to the back of the mat. Continue in this manner with the opposite edge of the opening and then the top and bottom edges.

7. Cut the large-print fabric to fit on the board behind the mat, centering your chosen motif in the opening. Mount with spray adhesive. Reassemble the frame.

For a quick frame fix, simply add a ribbon border to a square of large print fabric, cut background fabric or paper to fit the glass, and sandwich both between two layers of glass fastened with clips as shown above.

Gracie the Giraffe

Giraffe Grapes Gazebo Garden Gloves Garden Tools

G is for Growth Chart

How big is baby? Soooo big—and getting taller every day. Keep track with a growth chart that makes a special nursery accent. A nice touch: Choose letters that spell the child's name or initials.

Growth Chart

Finished size: 14x44-1/2"

Materials

◆ Preprinted alphabet block quilt panel

◆ 1-1/4 yard of green stripe fabric for sashing

◆ 1-1/3 yard of green print fabric for outer border and backing

◆ 1 yard of red check fabric for binding and ties

◆ 18x49" piece of lightweight quilt batting

◆ Air-erasable fabric marker

◆ Sulky® Rayon or Poly Deco™ Decorative Thread in red

◆ Sulky® Polyester Invisible Thread

◆ Sulky® Tear-Easy™ stabilizer

◆ Sulky® KK 2000 temporary spray adhesive

All measurements include 1/4" seam allowances. Sew with right sides together unless otherwise specified. The border strips are cut longer than needed and trimmed later to allow for individual differences in piecing.

Cut the Fabric

From quilt panel, cut:

    5—6-3/4" alphabet block squares

From green stripe, cut:

    2—1-1/2x40" sashing strips, with the stripes running the long direction

    6—6-3/4x1-1/2" sashing strips, with the stripes running the short direction

From green print, cut:

    1—17x48" backing rectangle

    1—3-1/2x40" right outer border strip

    1—1-3/4x40" left outer border strip

    2—3-1/2x15" outer border strips

From red check, cut:

    2—1x40" inner border bias strips

    2—1x10" inner border bias strips

    3"-wide bias strips to equal 135" for binding

    3—1-1/2x11" tie bias strips

Instructions

Assemble the Growth Chart Top

Diagram A

1. Arrange the alphabet block squares in a vertical row as desired. Referring to Diagram A, sew the squares together with 6-3/4x1-1/2" sashing strips and sew sashing strips to the top and bottom squares to complete the block panel. Press the seam allowances away from the block squares.

2. Measure to find the length of the block panel through the center as shown in Diagram B. Trim the two remaining green stripe sashing strips to this length. Sew the sashing strips to the left and right edges of the block panel. Press the seam allowances toward the sashing.

Diagram B

3. Measure to find the panel width through the center, including the sashing. Trim the two 10"-long red check inner borders to this length and sew to the top and bottom edges of the panel. Press the seam allowances toward the borders.

4. Measure the panel length through the center, including the inner borders. Trim the two remaining red check inner borders to this length. Sew the inner borders to the left and right edges of

the panel. Press the seam allowances toward the borders.

5. Using the measurement found in Step 4, trim the left and right outer borders to this length. Sew the outer borders to the corresponding edge as shown in Diagram C. Press the seam allowances toward the outer borders.

Diagram C .

6. Measure the width, including all borders. Trim the two remaining outer border strips to this length. Sew the outer borders to the top and bottom edges. Press the seam allowances toward the outer borders.

Embroider the Growth Chart

1. Refer to Diagram D to mark right outer border for embroidery. Measuring from the top edge of the growth chart, draw 1-1/8"-long lines at 1" intervals along the right edge of the outer border. Return to the top mark and lengthen that line to 1-5/8", indicating the 5-feet mark. Count down 12 lines and lengthen this mark for the 4-feet line. Repeat for the 3- and 2- feet lines.

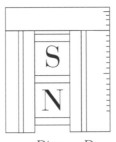

Diagram D

2. Pin the growth chart top, wrong side down, centered on the batting. Cut pieces of tear-away stabilizer slightly larger than the area to be embroidered. Use temporary spray adhesive to position the stabilizer on the back of the batting. Satin-stitch the foot and inch lines with red decorator thread as marked. Embroider 1-1/4"-tall numbers, 5, 4, 3, and 2, in front of the corresponding foot line with red thread. Tear away the stabilizer. For more information about embroidering, refer to "E is for Embroidered Accents" on page 28.

Complete the Growth Chart

1. Smooth out the backing on a flat surface with the wrong side up. Center the embroidered growth chart top, right side up, on the backing. Pin-baste the layers together.

2. Thread your machine with Sulky Polyester Invisible Thread in both the needle and the bobbin. Quilt in

the ditch along the outer edges of each alphabet block and along the outer edges of the sashing and inner border as shown in Diagram E.

3. Sew the short ends of the binding strips together with diagonal seams to form one long binding strip. Trim the excess fabric, leaving 1/4" seam allowances. Press the seam allowances open. Fold the strip in half lengthwise with wrong sides together; press.

Diagram E

4. Beginning at the center of one edge, place the binding strip on the right side of the growth chart top, aligning the raw edges of the binding with the raw edges of the top. Fold over the beginning of the binding strip about 1/2". Sew through all layers 1/2" from the raw edges, mitering the corners. Trim away the excess binding, leaving 1/2" at the end to overlap the beginning of the strip. Trim the batting and backing even with the growth chart top.

5. Fold the binding to the back of the growth chart to cover the machine stitching; press. Slip-stitch the folded edge of the binding in place or sew in the ditch along the binding, catching the folded edge of binding on the back.

6. Fold each tie strip in half lengthwise with right sides together. Sew with a 1/4" seam allowance, leaving the short edges open. Trim the seam allowance to 1/8", turn right side out, and press.

7. Pin the ties to the wrong side of the growth chart, with the center of the ties aligned with the binding seam. Place a tie 2" in from each top corner and at the center of the top edge as shown in Diagram F. Sew the ties in place along the binding seam.

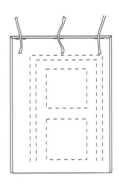

Diagram F

Harriet the Hippo

Hippopotamus Hen Hamburger Hat Hat Rack Honey Hibiscus

H is for Hibiscus Hats

Headed for Grandma's or the grocery? A handsome hibiscus hat tops off any outfit. Mix and match floral prints with gingham checks and stripes that coordinate with charming animals and alphabet letters.

Hibiscus Hats

Hibiscus Hats

Materials

- 1/2 yard of floral print fabric for hat

- 1/2 yard of coordinating fabric for lining

- Scrap of green print fabric for leaves

- Scrap of lightweight batting

- 30" length of 2-1/2"-wide bias strip of shiny red fabric for attached rolled flower

- Pattern paper

Trace the brim, top, and leaves patterns on pages 44-45 onto pattern paper and cut out. All patterns and measurements include 1/4" seam allowances. Sew with right sides together unless otherwise specified.

Cut the Fabric

From floral print, cut:

    1—3-1/2x21-1/2" crown

    1—7-3/4"-diameter circle for the top

    1 brim

From coordinating fabric, cut:

    1—3-1/2x21-1/2" crown lining

    1—7-3/4"-diameter circle for the top lining

    1 brim lining

From green print, cut:

    2 leaves

Instructions

1. Find the center of both long edges of the crown and mark for the center front. Sew together the short ends of the crown, making a circle. The seam is the center back. Bring together the center front and center back. Mark the folds for the sides of the hat. Repeat for crown lining.

2. Fold the top circle into quarters and mark the folds 1/4" from the raw edges as shown in Diagram A. Repeat for the top lining.

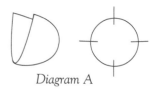

Diagram A

3. Pin together the top and crown, matching the marks and easing as necessary; sew. Turn right side out and press.

4. Repeat Step 3 for the lining. Press under 1/4" at the bottom edge of the crown lining.

5. Sew together the brim and brim lining, leaving the notched edge open. Trim the seam allowance, turn right side out, and press. Baste the open edge closed.

6. Pin the right side of the brim to the right side of the crown, matching the center back. The brim will overlap at the center front as shown in Diagram B. Sew the brim to the crown.

Diagram B

7. With wrong sides together, slip the lining into the hat, aligning the center backs. Pin the pressed edge of the crown lining over the brim seam allowance,

covering the stitching. Edge-stitch the crown in place as shown in Diagram C.

Diagram C

8. With right sides together, pin the leaves onto a scrap of lightweight batting. Sew 1/4" from the edges of the leaves. Carefully make a slit in the top leaf as indicated on the pattern. Trim the seam allowances, turn right side out through the slit, and press. Hand-stitch the slit closed. Machine-sew a line down the center of the leaves for the veins.

9. For the attached rolled flower, fold the 2-1/2"-wide bias strip in half lengthwise. Sew a row of gathering stitches through both layers a scant 1/4" from the raw edge. With the folded edge at the top, fold the right end down to extend 1/2" below the gathered edge as shown in Diagram D.

Diagram D

10. Roll the right end three or four times to create the center of the flower as shown in Diagram E.

Diagram E

11. Sew through the bottom several times to secure; do not cut the thread. Pull the gathering threads so the remaining ribbon measures about 12". Continue wrapping the strip around the center of the flower and securing the wraps at the bottom with thread. Referring to Diagram F, fold over the strip to cover the gathers. Tuck under the raw edges and tack in place.

Diagram F

12. Sew or glue the leaves and flower to the center front of the hat.

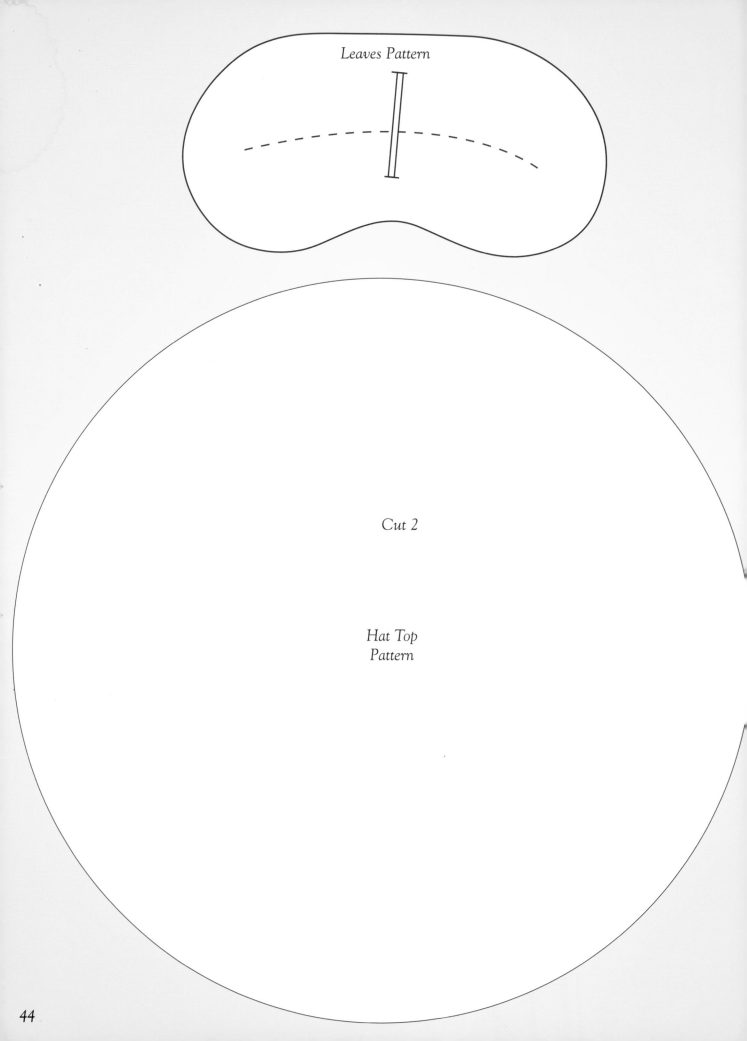

Leaves Pattern

Cut 2

Hat Top
Pattern

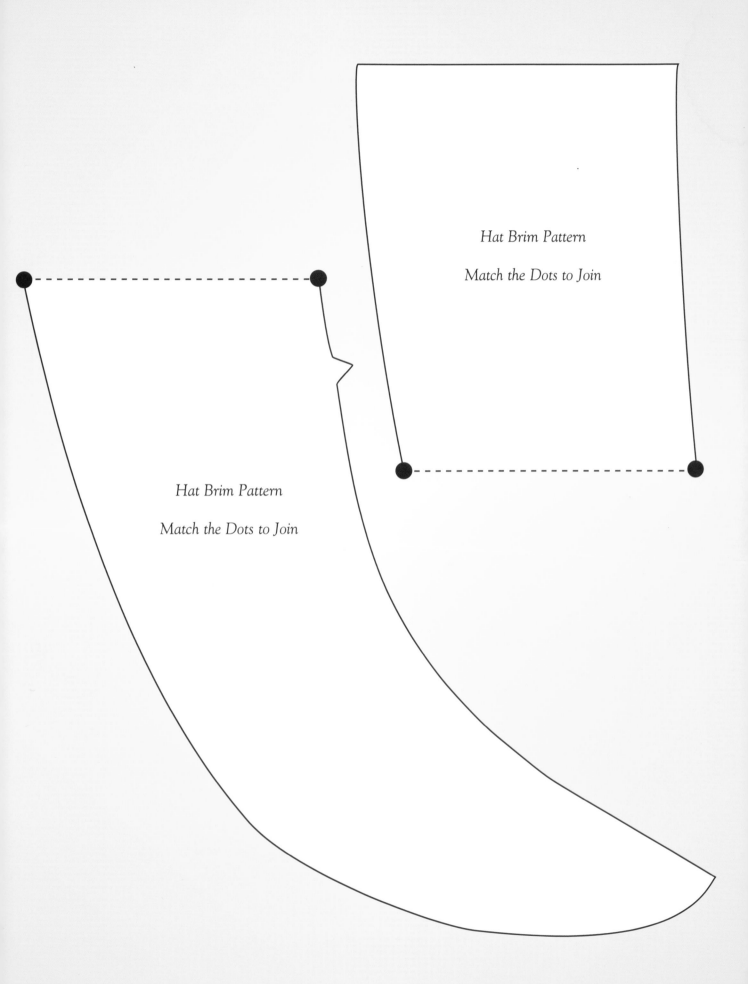

Hat Brim Pattern

Match the Dots to Join

Hat Brim Pattern

Match the Dots to Join

Irwin & Iris
the
Ice Cream Iguanas

I is for Invitation

Creating a personalized baby shower invitation is as easy as eating two dips of ice cream. Choose from charming Hungry Animals® from Janet Wecker–Frisch accented with beads on a string.

Invitation

Materials

- Purchased 5x7" blue card with white envelope

- Ruler

- 1-1/2x3-1/2" blue textured cardboard tag

- Yellow cardstock

- Red crafts wire

- White alphabet and heart beads

- Multi-colored floss

- Fabric scraps with desired motifs (our iguana is 5"-tall)

- Paper-backed fusible webbing

- Crafts glue

- Self-adhesive foam squares

- Pinking shears

Instructions

Make the Card

1. Make marks on each 7" edge of the card back, 1-1/2" from the top and bottom edges as shown in Diagram A.

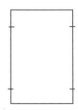

Diagram A

2. Line up the top marks with a ruler and draw a 1-3/4"-long line from each edge as shown in Diagram B.

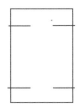

Diagram B

3. Draw vertical lines to connect the ends of the horizontal lines as shown in Diagram C. Cut on the lines through both layers, creating an I-shaped card.

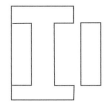

Diagram C

4. Draw around the blue cardboard tag onto yellow cardstock. Cut out the cardstock shape 1/8" inside the lines and glue centered on the cardboard tag. Wrap red crafts wire around the tag near the ends.

5. Thread the beads onto two lengths of multi-colored floss to say "You♥Are" on one length and "Invited" on the second length. Tie knots in the floss at each end of the beads to secure. Glue the bead strands centered on the yellow cardstock shape.

6. Cut out desired motifs from fabric, leaving about 1/2" around each motif, including a small motif for the envelope. Cut a corresponding shape of fusible webbing for each motif. Fuse webbing to the wrong side of each shape, following the manufacturer's instructions. Carefully cut out the shapes. Remove the paper backing. Fuse the shapes onto yellow cardstock. Cut out the cardstock about 1/16" beyond the edges of the fabric shapes, creating a narrow yellow border. Set aside envelope motif.

7. Refer to the photo to arrange the motifs and tag on the card front. Mount in place using self-adhesive foam squares for the tag and largest motif. Glue the smaller motifs in place.

Make the Envelope

1. Cut a piece of webbing the same size as the envelope flap and a rectangle of fabric slightly larger. Fuse webbing to the wrong side of the fabric, aligning the top edge of the webbing with a long straight edge of the fabric rectangle. Remove the paper backing. Fuse fabric onto flap, aligning the top edges.

2. Use a pinking shears to trim fabric just beyond the side and bottom edges of flap.

3. Glue the envelope motif to the center bottom of the envelope flap.

Jack the Jaguar

Jaguar Jam Jelly Jars Jugs Jungle Jumps

J is for Journal Cover

For wonderful memories, journal your baby's special days and new accomplishments. Tuck the journal into a colorful cover, and then use the "tucking" pockets for special keepsakes.

Journal Cover

Materials

◆ Approximate 9x11" journal

◆ Bumper border fabric for cover

◆ 2/3 yard of yellow stripe fabric for lining, end pockets, and piping

◆ 10x24" piece of lightweight batting

◆ 2 1/4 yards of narrow cotton cording

◆ Scrap of Sulky® Tear-Easy™ stabilizer

◆ Sulky® Rayon or Poly Deco™ Decorative thread in red

◆ Sulky® Polyester Invisible Thread

◆ Small "new baby" or "birth certificate" charm

All measurements include 1/4" seam allowances.
Sew with right sides together unless otherwise specified.

Cut the Fabric

From the bumper border, cut:
> 1—9-1/2x23" cover rectangle, planning the design placement

From yellow stripe, cut:
> 1—9-1/2x23" lining rectangle
> 2—6x9-1/2" end pockets rectangles
> 2—1-1/4x44" piping strips

Instructions

1. Referring to Diagram A, machine-embroider "Our Baby" or the child's name centered in the lower front area of the front cover using stabilizer and red decorative thread. For information about embroidering, refer to "E is for Embroidered Accents" on page 28.

> Our Baby

Diagram A

2. Center the cover fabric right side up on batting and baste 1/4" from cover edges. Thread your sewing machine with invisible thread and quilt as desired. Our cover was machine-quilted along the top of the clouds and bottom of the animals.

3. Sew the short ends of the piping strips together to form one long strip. Press the seam allowances open. Center cording on wrong side of strip and fold fabric over cording, matching long edges. Use a zipper foot to sew through both fabric layers close to the cording.

4. Beginning at the bottom edge of the back cover, pin piping to the right side of the cover, rounding corners with raw edges facing out and seam line of piping atop basting stitches. Clip seam allowance of piping at corners for a better fit. Overlap ends of piping, trimming off excess piping. Sew piping to cover using zipper foot.

5. Fold each 6x9-1/2" end pocket rectangle in half lengthwise to measure 3x9-1/2"; press. Pin, then baste the raw edges of the end pockets to the right side of the cover as shown in Diagram B.

6. Sew lining and cover together, leaving an opening at the bottom edge of the back cover for turning. Trim seams; clip corners. Turn cover right side out through the opening; turn pockets to inside. Press and sew the opening closed.

7. Sew the small charm on the front cover. Slip the ends of the book into the cover pockets.

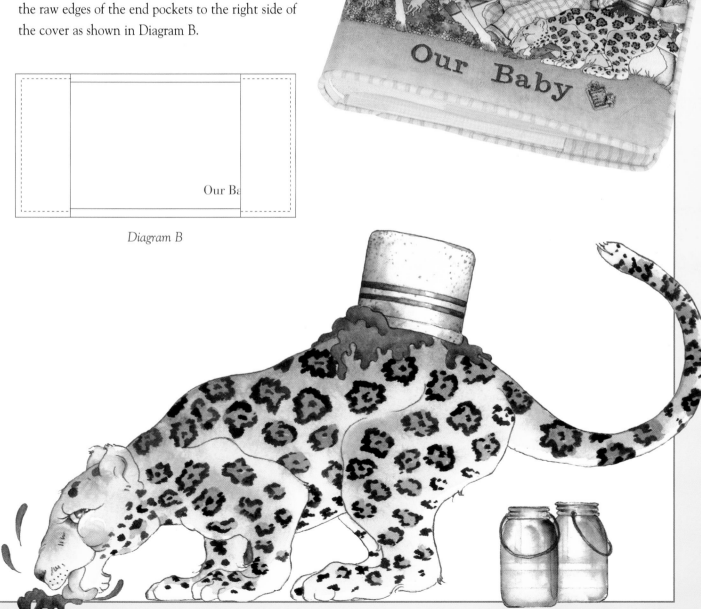

Diagram B

Katie the Kangaroo

K is for Kangaroo Kaddy

Almost everything you need when you change your little "Roo" is in the pockets of our "Kanga Kaddy." The kaddy fits over a square facial tissue box; the pockets hold items such as cotton balls, ear swabs and lotions.

Kangaroo Kaddy

Materials

- 5/8 yard of green stripe fabric for top, sides, pockets, and binding

- 1/4 yard of yellow small-print fabric for lining and pocket flaps

- 1/4 yard of red check fabric for pockets

- Large-print fabric with desired motifs for appliqué (we used two 4-1/2"-tall kangaroos)

- Paper-backed fusible webbing

- Sulky® Tear-Easy™ stabilizer

- Sulky® KK 2000 temporary spray adhesive

- Sulky® Rayon or Poly Deco™ Decorative Thread in red and yellow

- Sulky® Polyester Invisible Thread

- Air-erasable fabric marker (optional)

All measurements include 1/4" seam allowances. Sew with right sides together unless otherwise specified.

Cut the Fabric

From green stripe, cut:
   2—5" top squares
   1—18-1/2x5-1/2" side rectangle, with the stripes running the short direction
   2—6x10-1/4" pocket rectangles, with the stripes running the long direction
   1—1x20" binding strip, with the stripes running the long direction

From yellow small-print, cut:
   1—18-1/2x5-1/2" lining rectangle
   2—3-3/4" pocket flaps, with small motif in one corner

From red check, cut:
   2—6x10-1/4" pocket rectangles

From large-print fabric, cut:
   2—4x5" pocket appliqué rectangles, centering the motif

From fusible webbing, cut:
   2—4x5" rectangles

Instructions

Make the Appliqué Pockets

1. Fuse a rectangle of webbing to the wrong side of each 4x5" pocket appliqué, following the manufacturer's instructions. Remove the paper backing. Position a pocket appliqué centered along the bottom edge of each green stripe pocket rectangle as shown in Diagram A. Fuse in place.

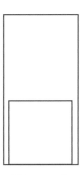

Diagram A

2. Cut pieces of tear-away stabilizer slightly larger than the fused rectangles. Use temporary spray adhesive to center a piece of stabilizer behind the fused shape on the back of each pocket rectangle. Satin-stitch over the left, right, and top edges of each pocket appliqué with red decorative thread. For an added touch, use yellow thread to machine-buttonhole stitch directly over the red satin stitching. Tear away the stabilizer.

3. Fold each green stripe pocket rectangle in half with right sides together to measure 6x5-1/8". Sew the raw edges together, leaving the bottom edge open as shown in Diagram B. Trim the corners, turn each pocket right side out, and press.

Diagram B

Make the Flap Pockets

1. Fold each red check pocket rectangle in half with right sides together to measure 6x5-1/8", in the same manner as for the green stripe pockets. Sew the raw edges together, leaving the bottom edge open. Trim the corners, turn each pocket right side out, and press.

2. Fold the pocket flaps in half diagonally with right sides together and the small corner motif away from the fold. Sew the raw edges together, leaving a small opening in one edge for turning as shown in Diagram C. Clip corners, turn each pocket flap right side out, and press. Edge-stitch along the two short edges of each flap, closing the opening with the stitching.

3. Position a pocket flap centered along the top folded

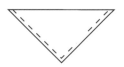

Diagram C

edge of each red check pocket. Edge-stitch the pocket flap to the pocket along the top edge as shown in Diagram D.

Diagram D

Assemble the Kaddy

1. Use an air-erasable fabric marker or machine-baste to indicate corners on the 18-1/2x5-1/2" green stripe side rectangle as shown in Diagram E. Measure 1/4" from one short edge for first corner line, then make a line every 4-1/2".

Diagram E

2. Pin the left edge of a flap pocket 1/8" from the first corner line on the side rectangle, aligning the bottom raw edges. Edge-stitch the left edge in place as shown in Diagram F, sewing through all layers. Pin the right edge of the pocket 1/8" from the next corner line, aligning the bottom raw edge. The pocket is wider than the space between the corner lines to allow for fullness.

Diagram F

3. Fold pleats at each bottom corner of the pocket to fit the pocket between the sewn left and right edges. Adjust the pleats so they are the same size. Referring to Diagram G, edge-stitch the bottom 1-1/4" of each pleat in place, sewing through all layers. Baste together the bottom edges of the pocket and side.

Diagram G

4. Repeat Steps 2 and 3 to attach the remaining pockets, alternating the flap and appliqué pockets on the side rectangle.

5. With right sides together, sew the 5-1/2" edges of the side rectangle together for a corner, stopping 1/4" from the top edge. Press the seam allowances open and turn so the pockets are on the outside. Sew together the 5-1/2" edges of the yellow small-print lining rectangle, stopping 1/4" from the top edge. Press the seam allowances open. Slip the lining inside the pocketed side piece with wrong sides together, positioning the seams at different corners to reduce bulk. Baste both the top and bottom edges together.

6. Press under 1/4" on one long edge of the 1x20" green stripe binding strip. Place the binding strip on the right side of the pocketed side piece, aligning the remaining long edge of the binding with the bottom edge of the side piece. Fold over the beginning of the binding strip about 1/2". Sew through all layers 1/4" from the raw edges. Trim away the excess binding, leaving 1/2" at the end to overlap the beginning of the strip.

7. Fold the binding to the lining side to cover the machine stitching. Slip-stitch the folded edge of the binding in place or sew in the ditch along the binding, catching the folded edge of binding in place.

8. Pin together the 5" green stripe top squares with right sides facing and the stripes running in the same direction. Mark the center on the edges with the ends of the strips. Referring to Diagram H, sew a 1"-long line from each mark toward the center of the square, backstitching to reinforce the ends of the seams. Fold each of the squares in half with wrong sides together along the center stitching lines to make the slit top. Press and baste the raw edges together.

Diagram H

9. With right sides together, pin the top edge of the sides to the slit-top, matching the corner lines with the corners of the top. Clip the seam allowances of

the sides/lining at the corners for a better fit. Sew the top to the sides as shown in Diagram I, taking care not to catch the top edge of the pockets in the stitching. To make a sharp turn at the corners, leave the needle down in the fabric, lift the pressure foot, and pivot the fabric. Clip the corners and turn the kaddy right side out. If corner lines were basted, remove basting at this time.

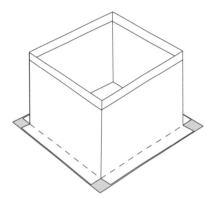

Diagram I

For a hop-to-it kwik kaddy, simply fill an inexpensive purchased plastic tote with baby's bath care essentials. Add a decorative ribbon bow and a gift tag created from the Katie the Kangaroo ornament as shown above.

Laila the Llama

Llama Lunch Lemons Lemonade Leeks Lace Lattice

L is for Lampshades

Lullaby time… The gentle rhythm of a rocker, the gentle glow of the nursery lamp…and your little one nods off. The peaceful scene is enhanced by an alphabet fabric print lampshade cover.

Lampshades

Materials

- Lampshade (our shade is 6-1/2"-tall with a 9" diameter)

- Large piece of pattern paper

- 1 yard of print fabric

- 1-1/2 yards of 1"-wide bias strips of coordinating fabric for trim

- Spray-mount adhesive

- Fabric glue

Instructions

1. Refer to Diagram A to make a shade pattern. Place the shade on its side on the pattern paper, with the seam facing down. Beginning at the seam, draw along the bottom edge of the shade as you roll the shade on the paper, until the seam is facing down again. Repeat for the top edge, keeping the bottom edge aligned with its line. Connect the top and bottom lines with a straight line for the seam. Cut out the pattern and wrap it around the shade to check the fit. Adjust the pattern if necessary.

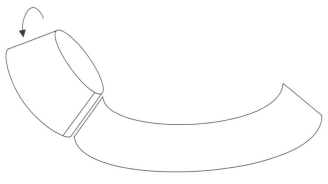

Diagram A

2. Pin the pattern onto the fabric. Cut out the shape 1/2" beyond the edges of the paper pattern.

3. Press under 1/2" on both curved edges and one straight edge of the shade fabric as shown in Diagram B.

Diagram B

4. Spray adhesive onto the shade, following the manufacturer's instructions. Smooth the shade fabric onto the shade, beginning with the raw edge of the fabric at the seam on the shade. Take care to align the pressed edges with the top and bottom of the shade. The pressed straight edge of the fabric will overlap the raw edge at the seam.

5. Carefully lift the pressed edges and secure in place with fabric glue.

6. To add trim, measure the circumference of the shade at the top and bottom. Add 1" to each measurement and cut a 1"-wide bias strip to each length, sewing the short ends of the strips together if necessary. Press under 1/4" on each long edge of the trim. Press the trim in half lengthwise to measure 1/4" wide. Glue the trim to the top and bottom edges of the shade. Secure the overlap with glue.

Let a little light shine on your creative talents!
Once you've completed the alphabet fabric print
lampshade cover, gather your decals,
paints, or rubber stamps and add some
animals and letters to the lamp base.

63

Marvin the Moose

Moose · Moon · Mountains · Milk · Muffins · Marshmallows · Mask

M is for Mobile

Round and round, with a happy tune, goes baby's own little carousel.
Soft blocks hang from a mobile frame, each block trimmed with rickrack.

Mobile

Materials

◆ Fabric with motifs to fill a 3" square for block sides

◆ 1/8 yard of small-print fabric for block tops and bottoms

◆ 1-1/4 yards of 1/8"-wide white satin ribbon

◆ 5—3x3x3" dense foam cubes

◆ Rickrack in coordinating colors

◆ Mobile

All measurements include 1/4" seam allowances. Sew with right sides together unless otherwise specified.

Cut the Fabric

From motif fabric, cut:
> 20—3-1/2" side squares,
> centering the motifs in the squares

From small-print fabric, cut:
> 10—3-1/2" top and bottom squares

Instructions

1. For each block, sew together four motif fabric squares as shown in Diagram A, starting and stopping 1/4" from the top and bottom edges and backstitching to secure the seam. Press seam allowances open.

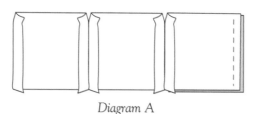

Diagram A

2. Position rickrack along the long edges on the right side of the block sides, as shown in Diagram B. Baste in place with the center of the rickrack on the 1/4" seam line.

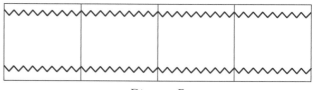

Diagram B

3. Sew together the remaining side edges of the first and fourth square, starting and stopping 1/4" from the top and bottom edges.

4. Sew a small print square to the top edges of the block sides as shown in Diagram C. To make a sharp turn at the corners, leave the needle down in the fabric, lift the pressure foot, and turn the fabric.

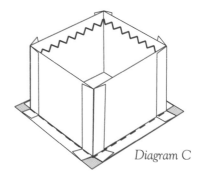

Diagram C

5. Sew a second print square to the bottom edges of the block sides in the same manner, leaving one edge open for turning as shown in Diagram D.

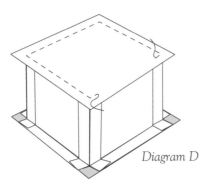

Diagram D

6. Trim the corners and turn the fabric block right side out. Tuck the foam cube into the fabric block through the opening. Whipstitch the opening closed.

7. Cut four 9" lengths and one 7" length of ribbon. Fold each ribbon length in half. Sew the ends of the longer pieces to a top corner of a block. Sew the ends of the shorter piece to the top center of the fifth block, making sure to catch some foam in the stitches to keep the fabric from pulling away.

8. Stitch, glue, or tie the folded ribbon ends to the arms of the mobile.

On an interesting note, the small fabric blocks suspended from the musical mobile are designed to detach and be used later as toy blocks (see page 100) when baby outgrows the crib mobile.

Ned, Nathan, & Norman
the
Numbats

N is for Nightlight

N is for "night-night." N is also for "numbat," a little Australian critter with a pocket. Put night-night and numbat together in this clever nightlight, and it's "Night-night, little baby! Night-night, little numbat!"

Nightlight

Nightlight
Materials

- ◆ Photocopy machine or computer, scanner, and printer
- ◆ Yellow cardstock
- ◆ Purchased nightlight with flat front surface
- ◆ Self-adhesive foam square

Instructions

1. Use a photocopy machine to copy the numbat of your choice onto paper. Or scan the image and print the numbat on white paper.

2. Cut out the numbat and lightly spray the back with adhesive. Press the cutout onto yellow cardstock. Cut out the cardstock a scant 1/8" beyond the edges of the fabric shape, creating a narrow yellow border.

3. Mount the shape on the front of the nightlight with a foam square.

Permission to copy is granted for your personal use.

Why limit yourself to nachos, neckties, and numbats?
Choose from any of the adorable Hungry Animals© featured as
ornaments or gift tags on page 75. Enlarge the critter of your
choice to fit the size of your nightlight.

Permission to copy is granted for your personal use.

71

Oliver the Ostrich

Ostrich Owl Oranges Olives Onions Overalls

O is for Ornaments

Oh, look! Ornaments on a feather tree for baby's first Christmas.
Or, use groupings of your favorite animal cut-outs from
paper or fabric to brighten walls or window shades in the nursery.

Ornaments

Materials

◆ Photocopy machine or computer, scanner, and printer

◆ Printer fabric sheets (optional)

◆ Coordinating cardstock

◆ 1/8"-wide white satin ribbon

◆ Spray adhesive

◆ Crafts glue

Instructions

1. Use a photocopy machine to copy the Hungry Animals onto paper, enlarging them as desired. Or scan the animals and paste the scanned images as needed to fill an 8-1/2x11" sheet. Print the animals on printer fabric sheets or paper.

2. Cut out the animals and lightly spray the backs with adhesive. Press the animals onto cardstock. Trim the cardstock about 1/8" beyond the edges of each animal, creating a narrow border.

3. For the hanging loop, cut a 5" length of ribbon. Fold ribbon in half and glue the ends to the top center on the back of ornament.

Choose from the following Hungry Animals© to make charming gift tags or use the large versions scattered throughout the book for ornaments to decorate baby's first holiday tree.

75

Patrick the Piggy

Pig Parrot Pancakes Pumpkin Porch Picnic Table Purple

P is for Pillows

If Patrick Piggy picked a pack of pillows,
How many pillows would Patrick Piggy pick?
Four styles—bolster, knife-edge, box, and ruffled square.

Pillows

Bolster Pillow

Materials

◆ 2/3 yard of bumper border fabric for pillow cover

◆ 1/2 yard of red check fabric for trim and ties

◆ 5x14" bolster pillow form

◆ 2 heavy rubber bands

Sew with right sides together using 1/4" seam allowances unless otherwise specified.

Cut the Fabric

From bumper border, cut:
  1—23x20-1/2" rectangle, with the design running parallel to the 23" edge

From red check, cut:
  2—7x20-1/2" trim strips
  2—6x22" tie strips

Instructions

1. Sew a trim strip to each 20-1/2" edge of the border rectangle. Press the seam allowances toward the trim.

2. With right sides together, fold the fabric in half lengthwise, matching the trim seams. Use a 1/2" seam allowance to sew the long edges together as shown in Diagram A. Turn the pillow cover right side out.

Diagram A

3. Fold in the red check trim at each end of the pillow, creating a 1/2"-wide red check border on the outside of the pillow and a 6-1/4"-wide lining on the inside. Press. To hold the lining in place, sew directly on the trim seam at each open end of the pillow as shown in Diagram B.

Diagram B

4. To make a tie, fold a 6x22" red check strip in half lengthwise with right sides together. Diagonally trim the strip ends as shown in Diagram C. Sew the raw edges together, leaving a 2" opening for turning. Trim the seams, turn right side out, and press. Sew the opening closed. Repeat for the second tie.

Diagram C

5. Insert the pillow form into the center of the pillow cover. Secure each end with a rubber band. Knot the ties over the rubber bands.

Knife-edge Pillow
Materials

◆ 1/2 yard of cream print fabric for outer border and back

◆ 1/2 yard of blue check fabric for inner border and piping

◆ Large-print fabric with motif of your choice for center square

◆ 2 yards of 1/4"-diameter cotton cording

◆ 16x16" pillow form

Sew with right sides together using 1/4" seam allowances unless otherwise specified.

Cut the Fabric

From cream print, cut:
    1—17" back square
    2—3-3/4x10-1/2" outer border strips
    2—3-3/4x17" outer border strips

From blue check, cut:
    2—2-1/2x6-1/2" inner border strips
    2—2-1/2x10-1/2" inner border strips
    2"-wide bias strips to total 68" of piping

From large-print fabric, cut:
    1—6-1/2" center square, centering your chosen motif in the square

Instructions

1. Refer to Diagram A to add the inner borders. Sew the 2-1/2x6-1/2" inner border strips to the top and bottom edges of the center square. Press the seam allowances toward the borders. Sew the 2-1/2x10-1/2" inner border strips to the left and right edges. Press the seam allowances toward the border.

Diagram A

2. Refer to Diagram B to add the outer borders. Sew the 3-3/4x10-1/2" outer border strips to the top and bottom edges of the inner border. Press the seam allowances toward the outer border. Sew the 3-3/4x17" outer border strips to the left and right edges. Press the seam allowances toward the border.

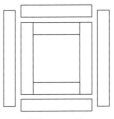

Diagram B

3. To make piping, sew the short ends of the piping strips together to form one long strip. Press the seam allowances open. Center cording on wrong side of strip and fold fabric over cording, matching long edges. Use a zipper foot to sew through both fabric layers close to the cording.

4. Beginning at the bottom edge of the pillow front, pin piping to the right side of the front, slightly rounding corners with raw edges facing out. Clip seam allowance of piping at corners for a better fit. Overlap ends of piping, trimming off excess piping. Sew piping to front using 1/2" seam allowance and zipper foot.

5. Sew the pillow front to the back atop the piping sewing line, leaving a 6" opening in the bottom edge.

6. Turn the pillow cover right side out. Insert the pillow form into the pillow cover. Sew the opening closed.

Box Pillow
Materials

◆ 1—6-1/2" block from preprinted alphabet block quilt panel for appliqué

◆ 1-1/2 yards of red check fabric for ruffle and sides

◆ 1/2 yard of floral print fabric for front and back

◆ 6-1/2" square of fusible webbing

◆ 9" square of Sulky Tear-Easy™ stabilizer

◆ Sulky® KK 2000 temporary spray adhesive

◆ Sulky® Rayon or Poly Deco™ Decorative Thread in white and red

◆ 3x12x12" box pillow form

Sew with right sides together using 1/2" seam allowances unless otherwise specified.

Cut the Fabric

From red check, cut:

    2—4x26" side strips

    4"-wide bias strips to total 200" of ruffle

From floral print, cut:

    2—12-1/2" front and back squares

Instructions

1. Fuse the webbing to the wrong side of the alphabet block, following the manufacturer's instructions. Remove the paper backing. Center and fuse the block on the pillow front.

2. Center the 9" square of tear-away stabilizer behind the fused block on the back of the pillow front with temporary spray adhesive. Satin-stitch over the edges of the block with white decorative thread. For an added touch, use red decorative thread to machine-buttonhole stitch directly over the white satin stitching. Tear away the stabilizer from the back of the pillow front.

3. For front ruffle, sew the short ends of 4"-wide ruffle strips together to form a 100" strip, then sew the remaining ends together to make a big circle. Press the seam allowances open. With wrong sides together, fold the strip in half lengthwise and press. Sew gathering threads through both layers 1/2" and 1/4" from the raw edges. Pull on the gathering threads until the circle of ruffle fits around the perimeter of the pillow front as shown in Diagram A, slightly rounding the corners. Adjust the gathers evenly, pushing a little extra into the corners of the pillow. Pin and baste the ruffle to the pillow front. Repeat to baste a ruffle on the pillow back.

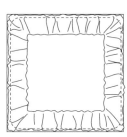

Diagram A

4. Sew the short ends of the side bands together to form one long strip. Press the seam allowances open and press under 1-1/2" at one end. Pin the side band to the right side of the pillow front, beginning with the pressed end at the center of the bottom edge. The opposite end will overlap as shown in Diagram B and the ruffle will be between the layers.

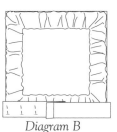

Diagram B

5. Sew the side band to pillow front as shown in Diagram C, sewing atop ruffle basting stitches, and clipping seam allowance of side band as you sew for a better fit.

Diagram C

6. Sew the opposite edge of the side band to the pillow back in the same manner, taking care to position the pillow back corners in line with the pillow front corners and leaving an 8" opening in the bottom edge. Pin together the overlapped raw edges of the side band to secure the band's correct length; baste in place.

7. Turn the pillow cover right side out. Insert the pillow form and sew the opening closed.

Ruffled Square Pillow
Materials

◆ 1 yard of yellow small floral fabric for outer borders and back

◆ 1 yard of blue print fabric for ruffle

◆ 1/8 yard of blue stripe fabric for inner borders

◆ 1—7" square block from preprinted alphabet block quilt panel

◆ 20x20" pillow form

Sew with right sides together using 1/4" seam allowances unless otherwise specified.

Cut the Fabric

From yellow small floral, cut:
    1—21" back square
    4—5-1/2x16" outer border strips

From blue print, cut:
    3—9x44" ruffle strips

From blue stripe, cut:
    4—2-1/2x9" inner border strips

From the alphabet block, cut into a 7" square

Instructions

1. Sew an inner border strip to the bottom edge of the 7" square alphabet block as shown in Diagram A. Begin sewing 2" from the right edge of the block and stop at the block's left edge. Press the inner border and the seam allowances away from the center.

Diagram A

2. Working in a clockwise direction, add the second, third, and fourth strips to the block as shown in Diagram B. Press all border strips and seam allowances away from the center. To finish inner border, complete the bottom seam, sewing from previous stitching to right edge of fourth strip.

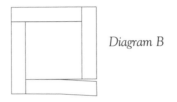

Diagram B

3. Sew the 5-1/2"-wide outer border strips to the inner border strips in the same manner, following Steps 1 and 2.

4. For ruffle, sew the 9" edges of the ruffle strips together to form a big circle. Press the seam allowances open. With wrong sides together, fold the strip in half lengthwise and press. Sew gathering threads through both layers 1/2" and 1/4" from the raw edges. Pull on the gathering threads until the circle of ruffle fits around the perimeter of the pillow front as shown in Diagram A, left on page 80, slightly rounding the corners. Adjust the gathers evenly, pushing a little extra into the corners of the pillow. Pin and sew the ruffle to the pillow front.

5. Sew the pillow front to the back atop the ruffle sewing line, leaving an 8" opening in the bottom edge.

6. Turn the pillow cover right side out. Insert the pillow form into the pillow cover. Sew the opening closed.

Queenie the Quail

Quail Quiche Quilt Quaint Quail Quiche Quilt Quaint

82

Q is for Twin Quilt

Guess what? Baby's quilt can have a big sister or brother, too.
Our twin-size alphabet quilt is a longer and wider version of our crib quilt.
Together, they're a charming coordinated set in a shared bedroom.

Twin Quilt

Finished size: 65x99"

Materials

- Preprinted alphabet block quilt panel for appliqués

- 1/3 yard each of check fabric in blue, green, pink, red, and yellow for center squares

- 1/3 yard each of small floral print fabric in blue, green, pink, and yellow for center squares

- 1/3 yard each of stripe fabric in blue, green, and yellow for center squares

- 2-1/4 yards of cream floral print for inner border

- 2-7/8 yards of blue print for outer border

- 6 yards of yellow large-print for backing and binding

- 73x106" piece of quilt batting

- Sulky® Tear-Easy™ stabilizer

- Sulky® KK 2000 temporary spray adhesive

- Sulky® Rayon or Poly Deco™ Decorative Thread in blue, green, red, white, and yellow

- Sulky® Puffy Foam™ in blue, green, red, and yellow

- Sulky® Polyester Invisible Thread

All measurements include 1/4" seam allowances.
Sew with right sides together unless otherwise specified.
The border strips are cut longer than needed and trimmed later to allow for individual differences in piecing.

Cut the Fabric

From quilt panel, cut:
- 8—7" alphabet blocks

From the 1/3 yard fabrics, cut:
- 9—12" letter squares (we cut 3 blue, 3 green, 1 red, and 2 yellow)
- 36—9" center squares (we cut 8 blue, 8 green, 8 pink, 3 red, and 9 yellow)

From cream floral, cut:
- 2—2-1/2x80" inner border strips
- 2—2-1/2x45" inner border strips

From blue print, cut:
- 2—9-3/4x102" outer border strips
- 2—9-3/4x48" outer border strips

From yellow large-print, cut:
- 1—44x103" backing rectangle
- 2—14x103" backing rectangles
- 3"-wide binding strips to total 9-1/2 yards

Instructions

Assemble the Quilt Center

1. Cut sixteen 12" squares of tear-away stabilizer. Use temporary spray adhesive to center two layers of stabilizer on the back of each 12" letter square. Machine-embroider a 4-3/4"-tall letter centered on each of the stabilized squares using decorative thread and matching Puffy Foam. Refer to the photo and Quilt Assembly Diagram for ideas on combining thread and fabric colors. Tear away the stabilizer. Trim each embroidered square into a 9" square, centering the letter. For more information

about embroidering, refer to "E is for Embroidered Accents" on page 28.

2. Lay out the center blocks on a flat surface, including the embroidered letter squares, in 9 rows of 5 blocks, using one letter square in each row. Arrange the blocks as desired or use the Quilt Assembly Diagram as a guide.

3. When you are pleased with the arrangement, sew the blocks together in rows. Press the seam allowances of each row to one side, alternating the direction with each row.

4. Sew the rows together to complete the quilt center.

5. For each alphabet block square, cut a 7" square of fusible webbing. Fuse webbing to the wrong side of each alphabet block, following the manufacturer's instructions. Trim each block into a 6-1/2" square and remove the paper backing.

6. Spread the quilt center right side up on a flat surface. Referring to the Quilt Assembly Diagram, position the appliqué blocks on the quilt, centering each over an intersection of four center squares. When you are happy with the arrangement, pin the blocks in place. Fuse the blocks to the quilt.

7. Cut squares of tear-away stabilizer slightly larger than the fused blocks. Center a piece of stabilizer behind each fused shape on the back of the quilt center with temporary spray adhesive. Satin-stitch over the edges of each block with white decorative thread. For an added touch, use a second color of decorative thread to machine-buttonhole stitch directly over the white satin stitching. Tear away the stabilizer.

Assemble the Quilt Top

1. Measure to find the quilt width through the center as shown in Diagram A. Cut two 2-1/2"-wide cream floral inner border strips to this length. Sew the inner borders to the top and bottom edges of the quilt center. Press the seam allowances toward the borders.

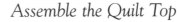

Diagram A

2. Measure the quilt length through the center including the borders as shown in Diagram B. Cut two cream floral inner border strips to this length. Sew the inner borders to the left and right edges of the quilt. Press the seam allowances toward the borders.

Measure

Diagram B

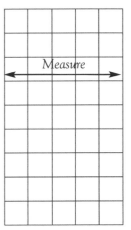

3. Measure to find the quilt width through the center, including the inner border. Use this measurement to cut two outer borders from the 9-3/4"-wide blue print strips. Referring to the Quilt Assembly Diagram, sew the outer borders to the top and bottom edges of the quilt. Press the seam allowances toward the outer borders.

4. Measure the quilt length through the center, including all borders. Trim the two remaining blue print outer borders to this length. Sew the borders to the left and right edges of the quilt. Press the seam allowances toward the outer borders.

Complete the Twin Quilt

1. Sew a 14x103" backing rectangle to each long edge of the 44x103" backing rectangle with a 1/2" seam allowance. Press the seam allowances away from the center of the backing.

2. Smooth out the backing on a flat surface with the wrong side up and center the batting on the backing. Center the quilt top, right side up, on top of the batting. Baste the layers together.

3. Thread your machine with Sulky Polyester Invisible Thread in both the needle and the bobbin. Machine-quilt through all layers beginning in the center and working out to the edges. Refer to Diagram C to quilt between the vertical and horizontal rows of center squares. Quilt around each appliqué block and in the ditch along the outer edges of the quilt center and the outer edges of the inner border. Quilt a 3" diagonal grid in the outer border.

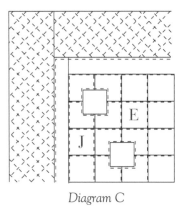

Diagram C

4. Sew the short ends of the 3"-wide binding strips together with diagonal seams to form one long binding strip. Trim the excess fabric, leaving 1/4" seam allowances. Press the seam allowances open. Fold the strip in half lengthwise with wrong sides together; press.

5. Beginning at the center of one edge of the quilt, place the binding strip on the right side of the quilt top, aligning the raw edges of the binding with the raw edges of the quilt top. Fold over the beginning of the binding strip about 1/2". Sew through all layers 1/2" from the raw edges, mitering the corners. Trim away the excess binding, leaving 1/2" at the end to overlap the beginning of the strip. Trim the batting and backing even with the quilt top.

6. Fold the binding to the back of the quilt to cover the machine stitching; press. Slip-stitch the folded edge of the binding in place or sew in the ditch along the binding, catching the folded edge of binding on the back of the quilt.

Your twin-size quilt can easily double as two when you make it reversible. Simply choose a coordinating large-print fabric such as the Hungry Animal Alphabet© shown here for the whole-cloth backing and the binding.

Twin Quilt Assembly Diagram

Roxie the Rhino

Rhinosaraus Racoon Raspberries Radishes Roses

R is for Rug

Start with balls of gingham-checked fabric strips ready to crochet into an unusual rectangular rug using an over-sized crochet hook.

Crocheted Rug

Crochet Abbreviations:

Beg = begin

CM = corner marker

ch = chain

RBM = row beginning marker

rd = round

sc = single crochet

sl st = slip stitch

sp = space

Crocheted Rug

Finished size: 20x30"

Materials

◆ 1 yard of green stripe fabric

◆ 3/4 yard of pink check fabric

◆ 1-1/4 yards of blue stripe print

◆ 1-1/2 yards of yellow stripe print

◆ Size N/15 (10mm) crochet hook

◆ 5 large safety pins or other markers

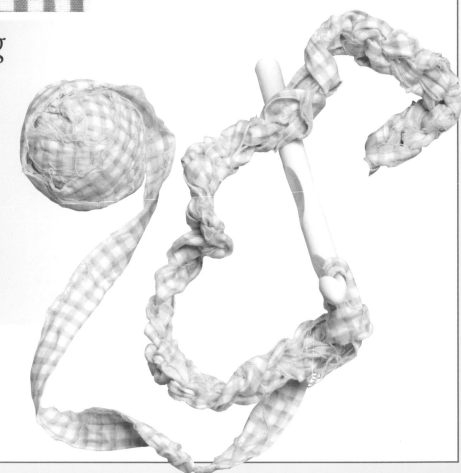

Cut the Fabric

From green stripe, cut:

    36—1x44" strips to total 44 yards

From pink check, cut:

    24—1x44" strips to total 29 yards

From blue stripe, cut:

    42—1x44" strips to total 51 yards

From yellow stripe, cut:

    54—1x44" strips to total 66 yards

Instructions

Prepare the Fabric

1. Make a buttonhole slit 1/4" from each end of each of the strips as shown in Diagram A.

Diagram A

2. To join two strips, place one end of the first strip through the slit in the second strip. Bring the other end of the first strip through the slit in the opposite end as shown in Diagram B, and gently pull until the first strip is knotted onto the second strip.

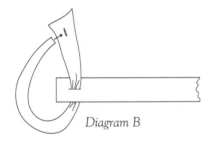

Diagram B

3. Continue adding strips until all strips of each color are joined. Roll each color into a ball, folding the strips in half lengthwise while you roll. To change colors as you crochet, tie ends in a square knot.

Crochet the Rug

Beg at rug center with green fabric, ch 11.

Rd 1: Skipping the first ch from the hook and working only in the back loops, 9 sc. In the last ch sc, ch 1, sc, ch 1, sc. In the front loops, 9 sc. In last chain, sc, ch 1, sc, ch 1, sc. Join with sl st.

Rd 2: Ch 1, place RBM in ch. Sc in each st to first ch 1 sp. [*Sc, ch 1, sc (corner made) Place a CM in first sc of corner. * Sc in next st. Repeat between**.] Sc in each st to next ch 1 sp. Repeat between [ ]. Sc to RBM, join to ch 1 with sl st.

Rd 3: Moving all markers to newly worked row, ch 1, sc to first CM. Make corner in first sc of corner. *Sc to next CM, make corner in first sc of corner. Repeat from * twice. Sc to RBM, join with sl st.

Rd 4: Repeat Rd 3. Change to pink fabric.

Rds 5–7: Repeat Rd 3. Change to blue fabric.

Rds 8–10: Repeat Rd 3. Change to yellow fabric.

Rds 11–13: Repeat to Rd 3. Change to green fabric.

Rd 14: Repeat Rd 3. Tie off at end of rd.

Sadie the Sheep

Sheep   Soup   Supper   Salt   Sugar   Stove   Spoon

S is for Shadow Box

Soft toys, tiny booties, a birth announcement, and other memorabilia of baby's earliest days are displayed in a shadowbox. The batting in the quilted background of patchwork blocks makes it easy to pin keepsakes in place.

Shadow Box

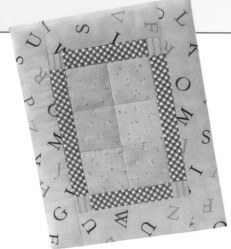

Quilted Shadowbox
Materials

◆ 11x14" shadowbox with rigid plastic insert

◆ 1/3 yard of green print fabric for outer border

◆ 1/4 yard of red check fabric for inner border

◆ Scraps of small floral print fabric in blue, green, pink, and yellow

◆ Scrap of yellow stripe fabric for border corners

◆ 11x14" rectangle of muslin

◆ 11x14" rectangle of lightweight batting

◆ Crafts glue usable with both fabric and plastic

◆ Memorabilia, such as photos, baby toys and clothing items

All measurements include 1/4" seam allowances. Sew with right sides together unless otherwise specified.

Cut the Fabric

From green print, cut:
> 2—4-1/2x18" outer border strips
> 2—4- 1/2x7-1/2" outer border strips

From red check, cut:
> 2—1-1/2x8" inner border bias strips
> 2—1-1/2x5-1/2" inner border bias strips

From small floral print scraps, cut:
> 6—3" center squares

From yellow stripe, cut:
> 4—1-1/2" inner border squares

Instructions

1. Arrange the 3" floral squares in 3 rows of 2 squares. Sew the squares into rows. Press the seam allowances of the top and bottom rows one direction and the center row in the opposite direction. Join the rows to complete the center of the shadow box backdrop as shown in Diagram A.

Diagram A

2. Refer to Diagram B to add the inner border. Sew a 1-1/2x8" red check inner border strip to the left and right edges of the center squares. Press the seam allowances toward the border. Sew a 1-1/2" yellow stripe square to each end of the 1-1/2x5-1/2" inner border strips, and then sew the pieced strips to the top and bottom edges of the center squares. Press the seam allowances toward the border.

Diagram B

3. Refer to Diagram C to add the outer border. Sew a 4-1/2x7-1/2" outer border strip to the top and bottom edges of the inner border. Press the seam allowances away from the center. Sew a 4-1/2x18" outer border strip to the left and right edges of the inner border. Press the seam allowances away from the center.

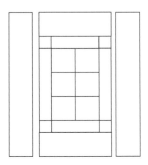

Diagram C

4. Overcast the raw edges of the pieced backdrop. Place the batting on the muslin rectangle. Center the pieced backdrop, wrong side down, on the batting. Pin-baste the layers together.

5. Machine-quilt between the vertical and horizontal rows of squares in the center and in the ditch along both edges of the inner border as shown in Diagram D.

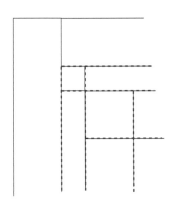

Diagram D

6. Center the plastic insert on the wrong side of the quilted backdrop. Fold the excess outer border to the back of the insert, mitering the corners. Glue the fabric to the back.

7. Arrange memorabilia on the backdrop. When you're pleased with the arrangement, glue or tack the items in place. Reassemble the shadowbox.

Fabric Shadow Box
Materials

- ◆ 11x14" shadowbox with rigid plastic insert
- ◆ 15x18" rectangle of blue print fabric
- ◆ 11x14" rectangle of lightweight batting
- ◆ Crafts glue usable with both fabric and plastic
- ◆ Memorabilia, such as photos and baby toys
- ◆ Embellishments, such as ribbon, buttons, and letters

Instructions

1. Overcast the edges of the blue print rectangle.

2. Place the blue print rectangle right side down on a flat surface. Center the batting on the fabric. Center the plastic insert face down on the batting. Fold the excess fabric to the back of the insert, mitering the corners. Glue the fabric to the back.

3. Arrange memorabilia on the fabric-covered insert. When you're pleased with the arrangement, glue the items in place. Add ribbon borders to the photos and embellish with button at the corners if desired. Personalize with the child's name.

Tim & Tami
the Toucans

Turtle   Tortoise   Toucans   Tea   Tray   Tablecloth   Trellis

T is for Toys

A-tisket, a-tasket,
A nicely filled toy basket.
This one holds a soft animal-filled ABC book and a set of soft blocks.

Toys

Toy Basket Liner
Materials

◆ Shallow basket or box

◆ Green check fabric for bottom and sides

◆ Red check fabric for trim

◆ Sulky® Tear-Eas™y stabilizer

◆ Sulky® KK 2000 temporary spray adhesive

◆ Sulky® Rayon or Poly Deco™ Decorative Thread in red

Sew with right sides together using a 1/2" seam allowance unless otherwise specified.

Cut the Fabric

1. Find the dimensions of the inside bottom of the basket; add 1" for seam allowances. Use these measurements to cut a bottom from green check fabric.

2. For the side strip, find the perimeter of the bottom from Step 1; add 2" for the strip length. Measure

from the inside bottom of the basket to the top edge; multiply this number by 1.75 for the strip height. This will allow for seam allowances and the embroidered turndown. Use these measurements to cut the side strip from green check fabric. Adjust the strip height as needed to result in the desired turndown and to allow enough space for embroidery.

3. For trim, cut enough 1"-wide bias strips to equal the strip length found in Step 2.

Instructions

1. Sew the short ends of the trim strips together to make one long strip. Press the seam allowances open. Sew the trim strip to one long edge of the side strip with a 1/4" seam allowance. Press the seam allowance toward the trim.

2. With right sides together, pin the remaining long edge of the side strip to the bottom, beginning with a strip end near the center of a bottom edge. For a better fit, clip the seam allowance of the side strip at the corners of the bottom as shown in Diagram A. Sew the side strip to the bottom, leaving about 3" of each strip end free. Reinforce the stitching at the corners.

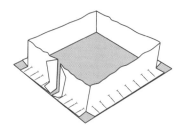

Diagram A

3. Place the liner in the basket to check the fit. Mark the seam location on the side strip, allowing the

side to become fuller if needed to fit over the basket. Trim the side strip ends, leaving a 1/2" seam allowance. Sew the strip ends together as marked; press the seam allowance open. Sew to complete the side strip/bottom seam, continuing the previous stitching lines as shown in Diagram B. Press the seam allowances toward the bottom.

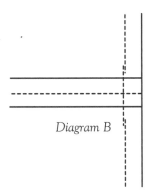

Diagram B

4. Machine-overcast the raw edge of the trim. Fold over 1/2" to the wrong side of the liner, creating a 1/4"-wide trim border on the front; press. To hem, sew through both layers in the ditch along the trim seam.

5. Machine-embroider "TOYS" with 1-1/4"-tall letters, centered on the front area of the liner using stabilizer and red decorative thread. For information about embroidering, refer to "E is for Embroidered Accents" on page 28.

6. Place the liner, wrong side down, in the basket. Fold the sides down over the outside of the basket so the turndown displays the embroidery on the front.

Large Fabric Blocks
Materials

◆ Variety of print fabrics

◆ Fabric with motif squares and rectangles for appliqué

◆ Paper-backed fusible webbing

◆ Sulky® Tear-Easy™ stabilizer

◆ Sulky® KK 2000 temporary spray adhesive

◆ Sulky® Puffy Foam™

◆ Sulky® Rayon or Poly Deco™ Decorative Thread in blue, green, red, white, and yellow

◆ Polyester fiberfill

Cut the Fabric

From print fabrics, cut:
    6—8" squares for each block

From motif fabric, cut:
    4 motif squares or rectangles for each block, leaving about 1/2" around each shape

Instructions

1. Cut four 8" squares of tear-away stabilizer. Use temporary spray adhesive to center two layers of stabilizer on the back of two 8" fabric squares. Machine-embroider a 3-1/2"-tall letter centered on each of the stabilized squares using decorative thread with matching Puffy Foam. Tear away the stabilizer. Trim each embroidered squares into a 6-1/2" square, centering the letter. For more information about embroidering, refer to "E is for Embroidered Accents" on page 28.

2. For each motif square or rectangle, cut a corresponding shape of fusible webbing. Fuse webbing to the wrong side of each motif shape, following the manufacturer's instructions. Carefully cut out the shapes. Remove the paper backing. Center a shape on each of the remaining 8" squares and fuse in place.

3. Use temporary spray adhesive to center an 8" square of tear-away stabilizer behind the fused shape

on the back of each square. Satin-stitch over the edges of the fused shape with white decorative thread. For an added touch, use a second color of decorative thread to machine-buttonhole stitch directly over the white satin stitching. Tear away the stabilizer. Trim each appliquéd squares into a 6-1/2" square, centering the appliqué.

4. Alternating letters with appliqué, sew together four squares for the block sides as shown in Diagram A. Start and stop the stitching 1/4" from the top and bottom edges, backstitching to secure the seam. Press seam allowances open.

Diagram A

5. Sew together the remaining side edges of the first and fourth squares, starting and stopping 1/4" from the top and bottom edges.

6. Sew an appliquéd square to the top edges of the block sides as shown in Diagram B. To make a sharp turn at the corners, leave the needle down in the fabric, lift the pressure foot, and turn the fabric.

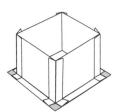

Diagram B

7. Sew the remaining square to the bottom edges of the block sides in the same manner, leaving a 3" opening on one edge for turning. Trim each corner as shown in Diagram C.

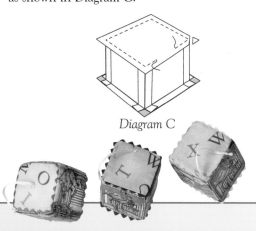

Diagram C

8. Turn the block right side out. Stuff the block with polyester fiberfill. Whipstitch or machine-sew the opening closed.

Small Fabric Blocks
Materials

◆ Fabric with motifs to fill a 3" square for block sides

◆ 1/8 yard of small print fabric for block tops and bottoms

◆ Rickrack in coordinating colors

◆ 3x3x3" dense foam cubes

All measurements include 1/4" seam allowances. Sew with right sides together unless otherwise specified.

Cut the Fabric

From motif fabric, cut:
   4—3-1/2" side squares for each block, centering the motifs in the squares

From small print fabric, cut:
   2—3-1/2" top and bottom squares for each block

Instructions

1. For each block, sew together four motif fabric squares as shown in Diagram A, starting and stopping 1/4" from the top and bottom edges and backstitching to secure the seam. Press seam allowances open.

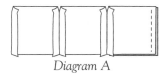

Diagram A

2. Position rickrack along the long edges on the right side of the block sides, as shown in Diagram B. Baste in place with the center of the rickrack on the 1/4" seam line.

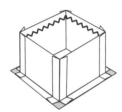

Diagram B

3. Sew together the remaining side edges of the first and fourth squares, starting and stopping 1/4" from the top and bottom edges.

4. Sew a small print square to the top edges of the block sides as shown in Diagram C. To make a sharp turn at the corners, leave the needle down in the fabric, lift the pressure foot, and turn the fabric.

Diagram C

5. Sew a second print square to the bottom edges of the block sides in the same manner, leaving one edge open for turning. Trim each corner as shown in Diagram D.

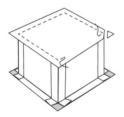

Diagram D

6. Turn the fabric block right side out. Tuck the foam cube into the fabric block through the opening. Whipstitch the opening closed.

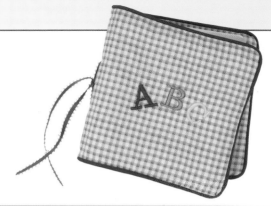

Soft ABC Book
Materials

◆ Preprinted alphabet block quilt panel for pages

◆ 1/4 yard of green check fabric for cover and lining

◆ 1/8 yard of green small floral print fabric for gusset

◆ 1 yard of low-loft polyester batting

◆ Air-erasable fabric marker

◆ Sulky® Puffy Foam™

◆ Sulky® Rayon or Poly Deco™ Decorative Thread in blue, red, and yellow

◆ Sulky® Tear-Easy™ stabilizer

◆ Sulky® KK 2000 temporary spray adhesive

◆ 1-1/2 yards of purchased narrow red piping

◆ 1/2 yard of 1/4"-wide red ribbon

◆ Tapestry needle

All measurements include 1/4" seam allowances. Sew with right sides together unless otherwise specified.

Cut the Fabric

From quilt panel, cut:
   20—6-1/2" alphabet block squares

From green check, cut:
   2—16x7-1/2" cover and lining rectangles

From green floral, cut:
   2—1x6" gusset strip
   2—1-1/2x6" gusset strip
   2—2x6" gusset strip
   2—2-1/4x6" gusset strip

From batting, cut:

> 1—15-1/2x7" rectangle
> 10—6" squares

From Puffy Foam, cut:

> 1—1-1/2x6-1/2" book spine

Instructions

The book is constructed of page sets, with each set containing four alphabet block squares. Most of the page sets use gussets at the center to accommodate the thickness of the pages.

Assemble the Page Sets

1. For Page Set 1, sew J to K/L and M to I in pairs as shown in Diagram A. Press the seam allowances open. With right sides together, sew the pairs together as shown in Diagram B, leaving a 5" opening centered on the bottom edge. Trim the corners and turn the page set right side out. Press, turning under the seam allowances of the opening. Insert two 6" squares of batting into the opening, smoothing one out on each side to reach the corners. Machine-sew the opening closed.

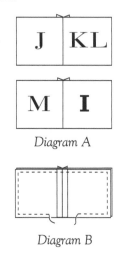

Diagram A

Diagram B

2. For Page Set 2, center the 1" gusset along the right edge of the H block with right sides together as shown in Diagram C; baste in place. Place the G block right side down on the H, sandwiching the gusset between the blocks. Sew the blocks together, catching the gusset in the stitching and leaving a 3" opening in the bottom edge. Trim the corners and turn right side out.

Diagram C

3. Center the opposite edge of the same gusset along the left edge of the N/O block with the G side up, as shown in Diagram D; baste in place.

Diagram D

Pin the P block to the N/O block with right sides together. The assembled G/H page will be between the layers; take care to keep it away from the seam line. Sew P to N/O, catching the gusset in the stitching and leaving a 3" opening in the bottom edge. Trim the corners and turn right side out. Press the assembled pages. Insert a square of batting into each opening, smoothing it flat to reach the corners. Sew the openings closed as shown in Diagram E.

Diagram E

4. For Page Set 3, center the 1-1/2" gusset along the right edge of the F block in the same manner. Sew E to F, leaving an opening for turning. Trim corners and turn right side out. Pin the opposite edge of the 1-1/2" gusset to the left edge of Q/R, sew S to Q/R, and finish the page set as in Step 3.

5. For Page Set 4, center the 2" gusset along the right edge of the D block. Sew C to D and turn. Pin the opposite edge of the gusset to the left edge of T, sew U/V to T, and finish the page set as in Step 3.

6. For Page Set 5, center the 2-1/4" gusset along the right edge of the B block. Sew A to B and turn. Pin the opposite edge of the gusset to the left edge of W, sew X/Y/Z to W, and finish the page set as in Step 3.

Assemble the Cover

1. To position the center of the embroidery on the front cover, mark a green 16x7-1/2 rectangle as shown in Diagram F with an air-erasable fabric marker. Measure 3-1/2" from top edge and 3-5/8" from right edge of cover.

Diagram F

2. Machine-embroider "ABC" centered on the marked area of the front cover using stabilizer, Puffy Foam and red, blue, and yellow thread. For information about embroidering, refer to "E is for Embroidered Accents" on page 28.

3. Beginning at the bottom edge of the back cover, pin piping to the right side of the cover, rounding corners with raw edges facing out and the stitching line of piping on the 1/4" seam line. Clip seam allowance of piping at corners for a better fit. Overlap ends of piping, trimming off excess piping. Baste piping to cover using zipper foot.

4. With right sides together, sew the cover to the cover lining atop the piping basting line, leaving a 6" opening centered on the bottom edge of the cover. Trim the corners.

5. Lightly spray temporary spray adhesive on the wrong side of the lining piece. Center and smooth the 15-1/2x7" batting rectangle onto the adhesive-side of the lining. Turn the cover right side out through the opening, encasing the batting. Press under the seam allowance of the opening.

6. For the spine, sew through all layers 7" from both the left and right edges of the cover to create a 1-1/2"-wide channel, sewing from the top to the bottom edges as shown in Diagram G. Slip the 1-1/2x6-1/2" strip of foam into the channel through the bottom opening.

Diagram G

7. Machine-sew the opening closed.

Complete the Book

1. Place Page Set 1 on Page Set 2 with J/K/L and H/N/O facing up. Line up the center seam of the top set with the center of the gusset on the bottom set. Sew through all layers along the center seam of the top page set as shown in Diagram H.

Diagram H

2. Keeping the same pages facing up, center Page Set 2 on F/Q/R. Turn the J page over and sew the gussets together along the right edge of the H page as shown in Diagram I. Then turn the pages over to the left to sew the gussets together along the left edge of the N/O page.

Diagram I

3. Repeat for the other page sets, placing F/Q/R on the D/T page set, and D/T on the B/W page set.

4. To attach the cover, center the B/W page set on the lining side of the cover. Sew the last gusset to the cover along the right edge of the B page and the left edge of the W page. These stitching lines should line up with the spine channel stitching lines.

5. Thread the tapestry needle with 1/4"-wide ribbon. Working from the outside cover, insert the needle through the spine 2-1/2" from the top edge of the cover. Bring the needle through the gussets, coming out between the J and K/L pages. Return the needle to the spine 2-1/2" from the bottom edge of the cover as shown in Diagram J. Tie the ribbon in a knot to secure, and trim ends to desired length.

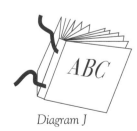
Diagram J

Ule & Vern
the Vultures

UV is for Ultimate Sheers & Valance

Combine customized sheers and an alphabet fabric border-strip valance for the ultimate in window treatments for the nursery that is urprisingly easy to make. Simply add fussy-cut fabric cut-outs to purchased sheers.

Ultimate Sheers & Valance

2. For each motif square or rectangle, cut a corresponding shape of fusible webbing. Fuse webbing to the wrong side of each shape, following the manufacturer's instructions. Carefully cut out the shapes. Remove the paper backing.

3. Spread the curtain panels right side up on a flat surface. Position the shapes on the panels. When you are happy with the arrangement, pin the shapes in place. Fuse the shapes in place.

4. Cut pieces of tear-away stabilizer slightly larger than the fused shapes. Center stabilizer behind the fused shapes on the back of the curtain panel with temporary spray adhesive. Zigzag-stitch over the edges of the shapes with invisible thread. Tear away the stabilizer from the back of the panels.

Ultimate Sheers

Materials

◆ Purchased sheer curtain panels to fit window

◆ Fabric with motif squares and rectangles

◆ Paper-backed fusible webbing

◆ Sulky® Tear-Easy™ stabilizer

◆ Sulky® KK 2000 temporary spray adhesive

◆ Sulky® Polyester Invisible Thread

Instructions

1. Cut out desired number of motif squares and rectangles from fabric, leaving about 1/2" around each shape.

Valance

Materials

◆ Bumper border fabric

◆ Green stripe fabric

◆ 3/4 yard of red check fabric for bias trim

Cut the Fabric

1. Measure the length of your curtain rod, including the side returns if they will be covered by the valance. Multiply this number by 1-1/2 or 2 to determine the finished valance width.

2. From the bumper border, cut enough 10-3/4"-wide border strips to total the finished valance width from Step 1. Depending on the amount needed, you may chose to purchase enough fabric to cut the valance in one piece or you can purchase less fabric and piece the bumper border to total the finished valance width. (The fabric shown has four usable borders per width of fabric.)

3. For the green stripe, divide the finished valance width number from Step 1 by 44, then round up to the nearest whole number to determine the number of fabric widths needed. Multiply this number by 11-1/4" (the width of the strips) to determine the amount of green stripe fabric to purchase. Cut enough 11-1/4"-wide strips to total the finished valance width.

4. For red check fabric, cut enough 1-3/4"-wide bias strips to total the finished valance width.

Instructions

1. If piecing the bumper border fabric, sew the 10-3/4" edges together to make one long strip. Press the seam allowances open.

2. Sew the 11-1/4" edges of the green stripe strips together to make one long strip. Press the seam allowances open.

3. Sew the short ends of the trim strips together to form one long strip. Press the seam allowances open. Fold the strip in half lengthwise with wrong sides together; press.

4. With right sides together, align the top edge of the bumper border strip with a long edge of the green stripe strip. Pin trim strip between the fabric layers, aligning the raw edges. Sew the raw edges together using a 1/2" seam allowance.

5. Machine-overcast the bottom edge of the valance. Press under 3/8" and top-stitch 1/4" from pressed edge.

6. For side hems, fold over 1/2" and then 1" on each short edge of valance; press. Edge-stitch close to inner pressed edges shown in Diagram A.

Diagram A

7. Press under 1/2" along the top edge of the valance. With wrong sides together, fold over 5" at the top of valance; press and pin. Refer to Diagram B to make the rod pocket, sewing 2" from the top fold and then 3" from the first line of stitching.

Diagram B

Wendall the Walrus

Walrus   Watermelon   Wingback Chair   Window   Winter   Willow Table

W is for Wall Quilt

Wow! This patchwork wall quilt really catches the eye and brightens any nursery. With the alphabet illustrated by blocks of whimsical Hungry Animals©, it becomes a visual aid for early learning.

Wall Quilt

Finished size: 43x50"

Materials

- 1 preprinted alphabet block quilt panel (ours measured 29x42" before trimming)

- 3/4 yard of red check fabric for inner border and binding

- 2-1/4 yards of blue print fabric for outer border and backing

- 46x56" of quilt batting

- Sulky® Polyester Invisible Thread

All measurements include 1/4" seam allowances. Sew with right sides together unless otherwise specified.

Cut the Fabric

For the quilt panel, trim 1/4" beyond the outer alphabet blocks.

From red check, cut:
> 4—2-1/2x44" inner border strips
> 5—2-1/4x44" binding strips

From blue print, cut:
> 1—44x54" backing rectangle
> 4—6x44" outer border strips

Instructions

Assemble the Wall Quilt Top

1. Measure the quilt panel width through the center as shown in Diagram A, and cut two 2-1/2"-wide red check inner border strips to this length. Sew the inner borders to the top and bottom edges of the panel. Press the seam allowances toward the borders.

Diagram A

2. Measure the quilt length through the center, including the top and bottom borders as shown in Diagram B. Cut two red check inner border strips to this length. Sew the inner borders to the left and right edges of the quilt. Press the seam allowances toward the borders.

Diagram B

3. Using the length found in Step 2, cut two outer borders from the 6"-wide blue print strips. Referring to Diagram C, sew the outer borders to the left and right edges of the quilt. Press the seam allowances toward the outer borders.

Diagram C

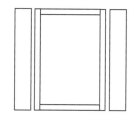

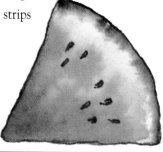

4. Measure the quilt width, including all borders. Cut two outer borders to this length from the remaining blue print strips. Sew the borders to the top and bottom edges of the quilt as shown in Diagram D. Press the seam allowances toward the outer borders.

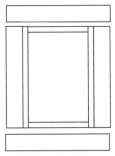
Diagram D

Complete the Wall Quilt

1. Smooth out the backing on a flat surface with the wrong side up. Center the batting on the backing and the quilt top, right side up, on the batting. Baste the layers together.

2. Thread your sewing machine with Sulky Polyester Invisible Thread in both the needle and the bobbin. Refer to Diagram E to machine-quilt between the vertical and horizontal rows of alphabet blocks and in the ditch along the outer edges of the panel and outer edges of the inner border. Quilt a 2-1/4" diagonal grid in the outer border.

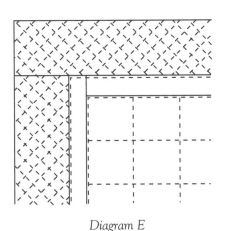
Diagram E

3. Sew the short ends of the binding strips together with diagonal seams to form one long binding strip. Trim the excess fabric, leaving 1/4" seam allowances. Press the seam allowances open. Fold the strip in half lengthwise with wrong sides together; press.

4. Beginning at the center bottom of the quilt, place the binding strip on the right side of the quilt top, aligning the raw edges of the binding with the raw edges of the quilt top. Fold over the beginning of the binding strip about 1/2". Sew through all layers 1/4" from the raw edges, mitering the corners. Trim away the excess binding, leaving 1/2" at the end to overlap the beginning of the strip. Trim the batting and backing even with the quilt top.

5. Fold the binding to the back of the quilt to cover the machine stitching; press. Slip-stitch the folded edge of the binding in place or sew in the ditch along the binding, catching the folded edge of binding on the back of quilt.

Zach the Zebra

Xylophone Yams Yardstick Zebra Zepplin Zucchini

XYZ is for X's & O's
Yards of Yo-Yo's
Zzz Baby's Sleeping

The Hungry Animal Alphabet's© done!
These final projects are fun: A game's X's and O's, And yards of Yo-Yo's.
Now the ZZZebra says your little one....is fast asleep. Sshh!

X's & O's Game

Materials

◆ 1/3 yard of green stripe fabric for board backing

◆ 1/8 yard of green print fabric for board border

◆ Variety of check and stripe fabric scraps for board center

◆ 1/4 yard of red check for board binding

◆ 12" square of lightweight batting

◆ Scraps of blue and green small floral print fabric for game pieces

◆ 1/8 yard of pale yellow synthetic suede or felt for game piece backing

◆ Sulky® Tear-Easy™ stabilizer

◆ Sulky® Rayon or Poly Deco™ Decorative Thread in red

◆ Sulky® KK 2000 temporary spray adhesive

◆ Paper-backed fusible webbing

◆ Pinking shears

All measurements include 1/4" seam allowances. Sew with right sides together unless otherwise specified.

Cut the Fabric

From green stripe, cut:
    1—12x12" board backing

From green print, cut:
    2—2x8" border strips
    2—2x11" border strips

From check and stripe scraps, cut:
    9—3" board squares

From red check, cut:
    1-1/2"-wide bias strips to total 55" of binding

From fusible webbing, cut:
    10—2-1/2" squares

Instructions

Assemble the Game Board

1. Arrange the 3" check and stripe fabric squares in 3 rows of 3 squares. Sew the squares into rows. Press the seam allowances of the top and bottom rows one direction and the center row in the opposite direction. Join the rows to complete the center of the game board as shown in Diagram A.

2. Refer to Diagram B to add the border. Sew the 2x8" green print border strips to the left and right edges

Diagram A

of the board center. Press the seam allowances toward the borders. Sew the 2x11" green print border strips to the top and bottom edges of the game board. Press the seam allowances toward the border.

3. With wrong sides together, layer the 12x12" green stripe backing and game board front with the batting in between. Baste the layers together 1/4" from the edges of the front.

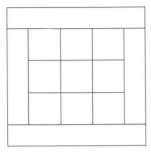

Diagram B

4. Machine-quilt between the vertical and horizontal rows of squares in the center of the game board and in the ditch along the outer edges of the squares as shown in Diagram C.

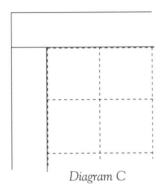

Diagram C

5. Sew the short ends of the red check binding strips together with diagonal seams to form one long binding strip. Trim the excess fabric, leaving 1/4" seam allowances. Press the seam allowances open. Fold the strip in half lengthwise with wrong sides together; press. Beginning at the center of one edge, place the binding strip on the right side of the game board, aligning the raw edges. Fold over the beginning of the binding strip about 1/2". Sew through all layers 1/4" from the raw edges, mitering the corners. Trim away the excess binding, leaving 1/2" at the end to overlap the beginning of the strip. Trim the batting and backing even with the game board top. Fold the binding to the back of the game board to cover the machine stitching; press. Slip-stitch the folded edge of

the binding in place or sew in the ditch along the binding, catching the folded edge of binding on the back of the game board.

Make the Game Pieces

1. Machine-embroider five 1-1/2"-tall Xs on blue floral print fabric and five 1-1/2"-tall Os on green floral print fabric using tear-away stabilizer and red decorative thread. Leave at least 3" of fabric between the embroidered letters. For information about embroidering, refer to "E is for Embroidered Accents" on page 28.

2. Draw a 2"-diameter circle on the paper side of each of the fusible webbing squares. Center and fuse a square of webbing on the back side of each of the embroidered letters, following the manufacturer's instructions. Cut out the letter circles on the drawn lines. Remove the paper backing.

3. Position the letter circles, webbing side down, on synthetic suede or felt backing, leaving at least 1" between the circles. Fuse the circles to the backing.

4. Cut a piece of tear-away stabilizer slightly larger than the area on the backing covered by circles. Use temporary spray adhesive to position the stabilizer on the back of the backing. Satin-stitch over the edges of the circles with red decorative thread. Tear away the stabilizer. Use a pinking shears to trim the backing about 1/8" beyond the satin stitching.

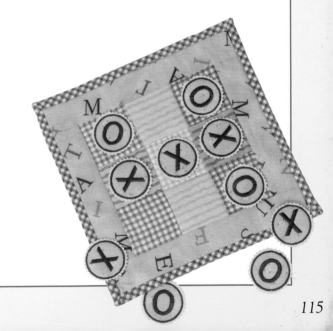

Yards of Yo-Yo's

Materials

◆ Variety of fabric scraps, measuring about 4-1/2"- and 6-1/2"-square

◆ 4"- and 6"-diameter objects, such as a saucer, lid, or compact disc

◆ Template plastic or lightweight cardboard

◆ Assorted buttons

◆ Fabric glue, optional

◆ 2—1 yard lengths of 1/4"-wide satin ribbon

Instructions

1. To make yo-yo patterns, draw around the 4"- and 6"-diameter objects onto template plastic or cardboard. Cut out the circle patterns.

2. Draw around the patterns onto fabric scraps and cut out the fabric circles. Plan on using 12 large yo-yo's for each yard of garland desired. Our garland has six large yellow yo-yo's followed either by a set of three small yo-yo's cut from different colored fabrics or else a single small green yo-yo. To save time, cut multiple circles from several layers of fabric at once, drawing only on the top layer.

3. To make a yo-yo, thread a needle with matching thread, bring the thread ends together, and knot. With the wrong side of the fabric circle facing up,

fold a scant 1/4" to the wrong side. Take small running stitches about 1/8" from the folded edge as shown in Diagram A. Continue to fold and stitch around the entire circle.

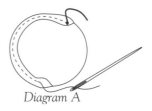

Diagram A

4. Pull the thread to draw the outside of the circle to the center with the wrong side of fabric inside the yo-yo. Pull the thread tight so only a small opening remains as shown in Diagram B. Knot and cut the thread. Flatten the yo-yo, centering the hole. Do not press. Repeat Steps 3 and 4 to make as many yo-yos as needed.

Diagram B

5. Sew or glue a button in the gathered center of each yo-yo.

6. To join the yo-yo's, place two together with the gathered front sides facing. Whipstitch the yo-yo's together with a few stitches along one side. Knot and cut the thread. To add a small yo-yo set, join three small yo-yo's first before attaching to the adjacent large yo-yo. Continue in your established pattern to complete the garland.

7. To hang the garland, sew the center of a ribbon length to the end yo-yo's. Use the ribbon to tie the garland in place.

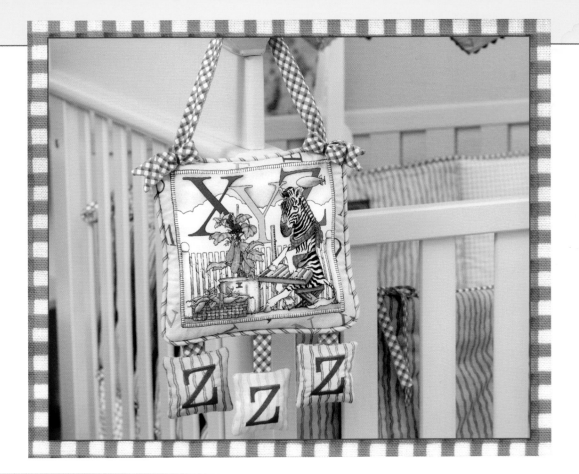

Zzz Baby's Sleeping
Materials

◆ 1/2 yard of red check fabric for door tie, bows, and letter hangers

◆ 1/3 yard of blue stripe fabric for backing, piping, and Z square

◆ 1/3 yard of green print fabric for front background

◆ 1—6-1/2x6" Z block rectangle from preprinted alphabet block quilt panel for appliqué

◆ Scraps of green and yellow stripe fabrics for Z squares

◆ 40" of narrow cotton cording

◆ 6-1/2x6" rectangle of fusible webbing

◆ 9" square of Sulky® Tear-Easy™ stabilizer

◆ Sulky® KK 2000 temporary spray adhesive

◆ Sulky® Rayon or Poly Deco™ Decorative Thread in white and red thread

◆ Polyester fiberfill

All measurements include 1/4" seam allowances.
Sew with right sides together unless otherwise specified.

Cut the Fabric

From red check, cut:
    2—2-1/2x18" bias strips for door tie, bows, and letter hangers

From blue stripe, cut:
    1—8-1/2x8" back rectangle
    1—5" letter square
    1—3" letter square
    1-1/4"-wide bias strips to total 40" of piping

From green print, cut:
    1—10" front background square

From green stripe, cut:
    1—5" letter square
    1—3" letter square

From yellow stripe, cut:
    1—5" letter square
    1—3" letter square

Instructions

Assemble Appliqué Pillow Section

1. Fuse the webbing to the wrong side of the Z block, following the manufacturer's instructions. Remove the paper backing. Center and fuse the block on the right side of the front background square.

2. Center the 9" square of tear-away stabilizer behind the fused block on the back of the background fabric with temporary spray adhesive. Satin-stitch over the edges of the Z block with white thread. For an added touch, use red thread to machine-buttonhole stitch directly over the white satin stitching. Tear away the stabilizer from the back of the background fabric. Trim the background fabric into an 8-1/2x8" rectangle, centering the Z block as shown in Diagram A.

Diagram A

3. Sew the short ends of the piping strips together to form one long strip. Press the seam allowances open. Center cording on wrong side of strip and fold fabric over cording, matching long edges. Use a zipper foot to sew through both fabric layers close to the cording.

4. Beginning at the center bottom edge, pin piping to the right side of the appliquéd front rectangle, rounding corners with raw edges facing out. Clip seam allowance of piping at corners for a better fit. Overlap ends of piping, trimming off excess piping. Sew piping to front using a zipper foot.

5. Sew front to blue stripe back atop the piping stitching line, leaving a 7" opening in the bottom edge. Trim seams; clip corners. Turn right side out through the opening.

Assemble Letter Squares

1. Cut three 4" squares of tear-away stabilizer. Center a green, yellow, and blue stripe 5" square each on a square of stabilizer with temporary spray adhesive. Machine-embroider a 1-1/2"-tall Z centered on each fabric square with red thread. Tear away the stabilizer. Trim each embroidered square into a 3" square, centering the letter. For more information about embroidering, refer to "E is for Embroidered Accents" on page 28.

2. With right sides together, fold one 18" red check bias strip in half lengthwise. Sew the long edges together. Turn the strip right side out; press. From the pressed strip, cut two 1-1/2" lengths and one 2-1/4" length for letter hangers, and two 4" lengths for bows. Set aside the bow pieces for later.

3. Baste a red check letter hanger centered on the top edge of each of the three Z squares as shown in Diagram B. Pin a same color square to each of the Z squares. Sew the squares together, leaving a 1-1/2" opening in the bottom edge. Turn the squares right side out. Press the squares, pressing the letter hangers away from the squares. Lightly stuff the squares with polyester fiberfill. Whipstitch the openings closed.

Diagram B

118

Complete the Door Hanger

1. Pin the red check letter hangers to the bottom edge of the appliquéd front as shown in Diagram C. Center the longer hanger and position the shorter two hangers 2" away. Sew the hangers to the front only. Stuff the appliqué pillow with polyester fiberfill. Whipstitch the opening closed.

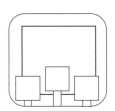

Diagram C

2. For door tie, fold the remaining red check bias strip in half lengthwise with right sides together. Mark the ends as shown in Diagram D. Sew on the marked lines and the long raw edges, leaving a 2" opening for turning. Trim seams, turn right side out, and press. Whipstitch the opening closed. Tack the door tie to the front of the appliqué pillow, 1" from each top corner and 2" from the tie ends to create bow tails.

Diagram D

3. For the bows, use the set aside red bias strips. Fold each strip so the ends overlap at the center back as shown in Diagram E to form a 1-3/4"-wide bow. Wrap red thread around the center to secure. Sew the bows to the door tie, covering the tack stitches.

Diagram E